KNITTING BASICS

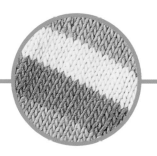

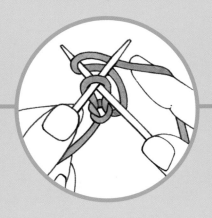

KNITTING BASICS

All you need to know to take up your needles and get knitting

Betty Barnden

A QUARTO BOOK

First edition for the United States, its territories and dependencies, and Canada published in 2002 by Barron's Educational Series, Inc.

All inquiries should be addressed to:
Barron's Educational Series, Inc.
250 Wireless Boulevard
Hauppauge, New York 11788
http://www.barronseduc.com

International Standard Book No. 0-7641-5546-6

Library of Congress Catalog Card No. 2001098710

Conceived, designed, and produced by
Quarto Publishing plc
The Old Brewery
6 Blundell Street
London N7 9BH

QUAR.KBA

Project editor Nadia Naqib
Art editor Karla Jennings
Designer Michelle Canatella
Illustrator Coral Mula
Text editors Sue Whiting, Kate Phelps
Pattern checker Pauline Hornsby
Assistant art director Penny Cobb
Photographer Paul Forrester
Indexer Pamela Ellis

Art director Moira Clinch
Publisher Piers Spence

Manufactured by Universal Graphics
Pte Ltd Singapore

Printed by Leefung-Asco Printers Ltd, China

9 8 7 6 5 4 3 2 1

CONTENTS

Introduction   6

GETTING STARTED

○ Materials   10

○ Basic Skills   16

PROJECTS AND TECHNIQUES

○ Combining Knit and Purl   34

   PROJECT 1: Striped Garter Scarf   38

○ Finishing   40

   PROJECT 2: Baby Afghan   48

○ Gauge   50

○ Working from Patterns   52

   PROJECT 3: Tank Top   60

○ Shaping   62

   PROJECT 4: Family Sweater   72

○ Knitting in the Round   74

   PROJECT 5: Sweater and Hat   77

○ Details   81

   PROJECT 6: Toddler Top   86

○ Stitch Library   89

   PROJECT 7: Lady's Lacy Vest   94

   PROJECT 8: Cable Cushion   105

○ Fair Isle (Two-Color Knitting)   107

   PROJECT 9: Fair Isle Sweater   110

○ Intarsia (Picture Knitting)   114

○ Finishing Touches   117

   PROJECT 10: Child's Sweater   122

○ Glossary   126

○ Abbreviations and Symbols   127

○ Index   128

INTRODUCTION

Knitting is a wonderfully flexible art: it's fun to work and the results can be as practical or as creative as you wish. Once you have learned a few basic skills, you can create warm, soft, easy-to-wear garments (and other items too) in exciting textures and color combinations.

This book shows you how to knit from the very beginning, step-by-step, progressing from the elementary stitches through to a variety of interesting techniques. Begin by learning how to cast on, knit, purl, and bind off. When you have mastered these basics, learn to work textured stitch patterns, Fair Isle and picture knitting, and how to shape and finish a garment. Each topic is fully explained and illustrated, showing clearly how to work the basic stitch formations and other techniques. Knitting has a long and varied history, and different techniques have developed at various times in different parts of the world, so sometimes there are several ways of working to achieve the same result. In these cases, this book describes the simplest method, or a method in common use today. You may discover other ways of working for yourself, or learn from other knitters.

Along the way, projects for practical and stylish garments, accessories, and articles for the home give you the opportunity to use each technique as you learn it. If you work through the book in order, you will find that the projects at each stage use only those stitches and methods you have already learned. Read the

book with yarn and needles close at hand, making small test-pieces to try out each technique, and then if you wish, make the project following each section. By the end of the book you will have acquired all the basic skills needed to pursue this fascinating, relaxing, and creative craft.

Knitting is an ideal hobby in today's busy world: it can be laid aside and picked up again at any time, requires little special equipment, and is easy to carry around with you. The new hand-knitter will find today's super-chunky and bulky yarns ideal for achieving quick results, and the new generation of micro-fiber yarns unsurpassed for comfort and practicality. The wide range of beautiful colors and textures, styles and patterns currently available will surely inspire you to pick up your needles, and with the help of this book you will be able to follow any pattern. You can then create original garments for yourself and your family by choosing your own color combinations and adding your own individual touches.

As you pursue your new craft and the basic skills become familiar, you will find that knitting can be relaxing and satisfying, as well as productive. Enjoy the colors and textures, let the rhythm of the needles take over your fingers, and watch your work grow in your hands.

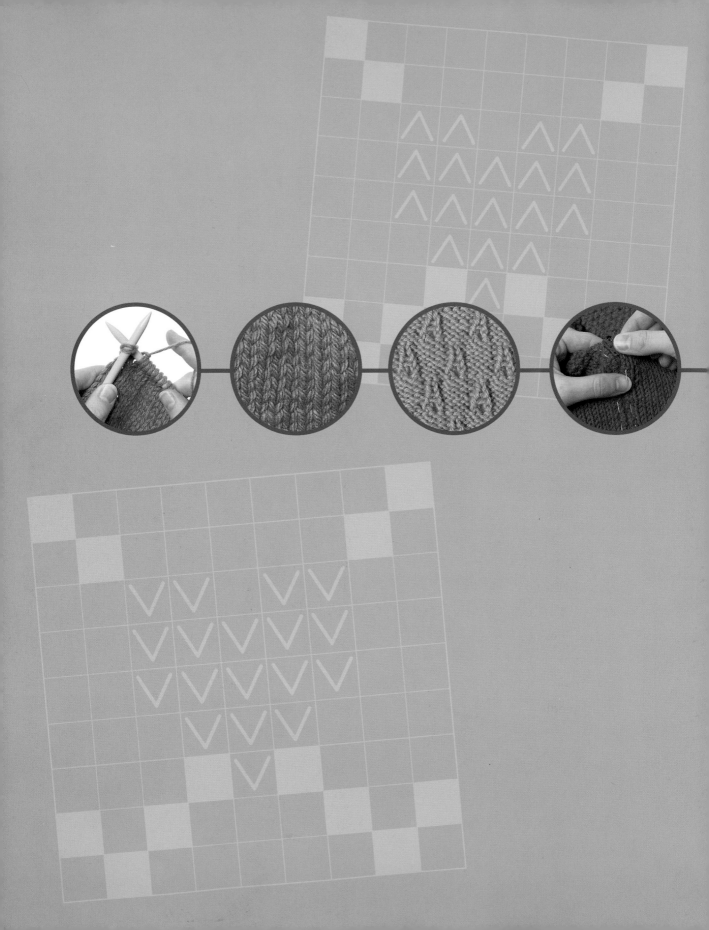

GETTING STARTED

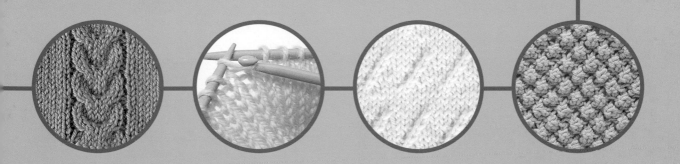

In this section you will find all the information you need to start knitting including how to choose suitable yarns and needles, a description of any other equipment you may need, and clear step-by-step instructions on how to work the basic stitches. The four fundamental elements of knitting are described and illustrated: how to begin by casting on stitches, how to knit, how to purl, and how to bind off when you have finished your knitted piece. These techniques will form the basis of all the knitting you will ever make in the future. Once you have learned and practiced these basic movements, you will be ready to tackle your very first project. So pick up your needles and start knitting!

MATERIALS

Knitting requires only two basic elements: a ball of yarn and a pair of needles, but it is important to choose the right yarn for a project, and the right needles to suit the yarn. Other equipment, such as pins and scissors, are common household items, but as you pursue your new hobby you may find it helpful to buy other accessories (page 15).

YARN

Knitting yarns are usually made by spinning fibers together. These fibers may be natural or synthetic, and the type of fiber will affect the performance of the yarn: its warmth, strength, softness, and stretchability.

NATURAL FIBERS

Animal products Wool (from sheep), mohair and cashmere (from goats), angora (from angora rabbits), alpaca, vicuna, and other animal hairs are shorn or combed from the animal before being spun into yarn. Animal fibers in general are light, soft, and recover their shape well after stretching. They are also good insulators, making them warm to wear. They may be spun together with other fibers to improve their strength and reduce the cost. Silk yarn is also a natural product, spun from the unwound cocoons of the silkworm. It is a good insulator and may be spun very finely but has little resilience and therefore tends to stretch in wear.

Vegetable products Cotton, linen, and ramie are derived from plants. They are cool, smooth, and wash well but tend to lack resilience and so are often blended with other fibers. Mercerized cotton is chemically treated to make it more lustrous and less liable to shrink. Rayon is also a vegetable-based product but the fiber is man-made, being derived from cellulose, a waste product of the wood and cotton industries. It is lustrous and soft but lacks elasticity and is often combined with other fibers for its decorative properties.

SYNTHETIC FIBERS

Acrylic, polyester, polyamide (nylon), and other synthetic fibers are derived from coal and petroleum products and spun in various ways to resemble natural fiber yarns. Such yarns are generally inexpensive, stable, and often machine washable. However, care should be taken when pressing or blocking these yarns; garments made from them will lose their shape if too much heat is applied. Many blended yarns are designed to combine the desirable properties of synthetic and natural fibers.

YARN TYPES

Fibers are normally twisted together by spinning them. Different combinations and methods produce different types of yarn: thick and thin strands may be spun together, or two threads spun at different tensions to produce a variety of textured effects. Different fibers may also be combined: matte cotton with lustrous rayon, or slubby (alternately thick and thin) wool with smooth acrylic. There id a huge number of possible combinations. Strands of different colors may also be introduced, or yarns may be space-dyed (random-dyed) with several different shades in the same ball. Other yarns are constructed in different ways. Chenille-type yarns are made by trapping short pile threads

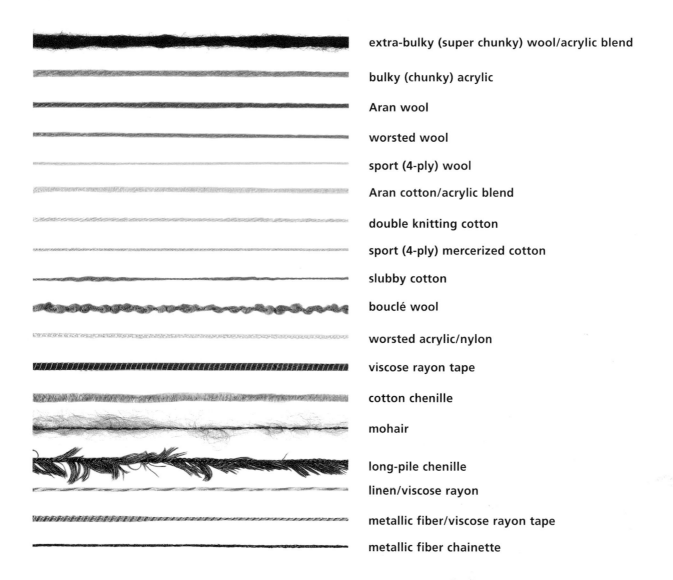

extra-bulky (super chunky) wool/acrylic blend

bulky (chunky) acrylic

Aran wool

worsted wool

sport (4-ply) wool

Aran cotton/acrylic blend

double knitting cotton

sport (4-ply) mercerized cotton

slubby cotton

bouclé wool

worsted acrylic/nylon

viscose rayon tape

cotton chenille

mohair

long-pile chenille

linen/viscose rayon

metallic fiber/viscose rayon tape

metallic fiber chainette

in a tightly twisted central core; tape yarns, ribbon yarns, and chainette yarns often consist of continuous threads knitted into fine tubes, flattened or rounded in profile.

Yarn weights

Yarns are available in many different "weights" (thicknesses), from extra-bulky to very fine. The names given above to these various weights are only a guideline as the terms used by different manufacturers, and in different countries, do not always correspond.

BALLS AND HANKS

Yarn is sold by weight, usually in balls of 1¾ oz (50 g) or 3½ oz (100 g).
Yarn supplied in hanks must be wound into balls before knitting.

WINDING A HANK

STEP 1
Untwist the hank and remove the tying threads used to secure it. Stretch it firmly several times between your hands to remove any kinks.

STEP 2
Ask another person to hold the skein in the same way as above or place it over a chair back to prevent tangling.

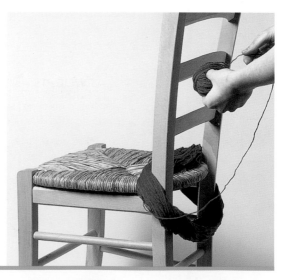

STEP 3 Find the
outside end of the yarn and begin to wind it around four fingers. Change the direction of the winding from time to time to keep the ball even. Always wind over four fingers so that when the fingers are released, the yarn is loosely wound and not stretched.

TIP
Keep a ball-band from each project as a future reference for washing and pressing instructions.

TIP
Keep unused balls of yarn away from dust and damp by storing them in a plastic bag. Odds and ends from previous projects may be sorted by weight, fiber content, and color in transparent plastic bags or boxes. An organized collection of odd balls and remnants can help you find just the touch of contrast color you need for a future project.

YARN LABELS

Most yarn is sold with an accompanying label or ball-band, giving the following information: weight of ball or hank, fiber content, washing and pressing instructions, recommended needle size (it is a good rule never to change the recommended needle size by more than two sizes), and recommended gauge (page 50). An approximate length is often quoted in yards or meters.

The shade of the yarn will be named and/or numbered and accompanied by a **dye lot number**. Yarn is dyed in batches, or dye lots, and the color may vary slightly from one batch to another. Such a variation will be very obvious when the yarn is knitted up, so always try to purchase all the yarn for a garment at the same time and check that all the balls carry the same dye lot number.

EQUIVALENT WEIGHTS AND MEASURES

U.S.	OTHER
1 oz	28 g
2 oz	57 g
1¾ oz	50 g
3½ oz	100 g
1 in.	2.5 cm
4 in.	10 cm
1 yard	91.4 cm
39½ in.	1 m

NEEDLES

TIP

Thrift shops are a great source for knitting needles, but beware! Before the introduction of sizing in millimeters (mm), UK and Canadian sizes were numbered from 14 (small) to 000 (large), unlike U.S. sizes which are numbered from 0 (small) to 19 (large). Avoid any potential pitfalls by investing in a needle gauge (page 15) to check the needle sizes.

Pairs of needles come in a range of sizes, from large (size 19 [15 mm]) to fine (size 0 [2 mm]), to suit different weights of yarn. They are also commonly available in different lengths, from 8 in. (20 cm) to 16 in. (40 cm), to suit the number of stitches required.

Double-pointed needles are sold in sets of four or five in the same range of sizes and various lengths. These are used for knitting in the round (page 74).

Circular needles are also used for knitting in the round, particularly with large numbers of stitches (page 74). They consist of rigid tips joined by a flexible cord.

Single and double-pointed and circular needles may be plastic, aluminum, wood, bamboo, or steel. Larger sizes are normally plastic or wood for lightness, and very small sizes aluminum or steel for strength.

NEEDLE CARE
Needles should be kept clean and dry and stored flat with the points protected. Plastic and aluminum needles may be washed in warm water if they become greasy. Damaged needles will snag the yarn as you knit—replace them.

EQUIVALENT NEEDLE SIZES	
U.S.	**OTHER**
19	15 mm
17	12 or 13 mm
15	10 mm
13	9 mm
11	8 mm
	7½ mm
	7 mm
10½	6½ mm
10	6 mm
9	5½ mm
8	5 mm
7	4½ mm
6	4 mm
5	3¾ mm
4	3½ mm
3	3¼ mm
	3 mm
2	2¾ mm
	2½ mm
1	2¼ mm
0	2 mm

OTHER EQUIPMENT

There are a few items you may need to complete your knitting projects.

Plastic bobbins Used to hold small amounts of yarn; particularly useful for intarsia knitting (pages 114–116).

Needle gauge To check the size of any knitting needle.

Cable needles Used when working cables (pages 96–97).

Crochet hooks Two or three different sizes, used to correct mistakes (pages 57–58).

Row counters Fit one close to the knob of a single-point needle to help you keep count of the rows as they are completed.

Tape measure Buy a new one from time to time, as old tape measures stretch with use and become inaccurate.

Stitch holders Used for temporarily holding stitches (see page 56).

Ring markers Split rings of plastic or metal to slip into the knitting, or onto a needle, to mark a particular stitch or row.

Yarn needles These should have large eyes and blunt tips to prevent splitting strands of yarn. They are available in different sizes to suit varying weights of yarn; tapestry needles may be used for fine yarns.

Small sharp scissors Used to cut the yarn.

Mohair brush (teasel brush) Used to raise the pile on a mohair garment after completion.

Point protectors Useful when storing or transporting work in progress, or to store needles.

Large-headed pins To hold knitted pieces as you sew them together. Large heads help you to see the pins in the knitting; ordinary dressmakers' pins are easily lost between the stitches.

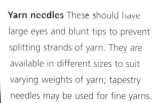

Basic skills

Choosing yarn and needles

Choose suitable yarn and needles to practice the basic skills described in this section.

When knitting for the first time, it is advisable to use a medium- to heavy-weight yarn, such as worsted or Aran (fisherman), or a bulky-weight yarn, with a plain, smooth finish so that you can see the stitches easily. More elaborate yarns can be confusing at this early stage. You will also need a pair of suitably sized needles. Many yarns quote recommended needle sizes on the ball-bands; choose the largest recommended size.

Here is a general guide to recommended needle sizes, depending on the yarn used:

WORSTED YARN	size 6 or 7 (4 or 4½ mm)
ARAN (FISHERMAN) YARN	size 8 or 9 (5 or 5½ mm)
BULKY YARN	size 10 or 10½ (6 or 6½ mm)

Shorter-length needles are easier to handle than longer ones; 10 in. (25 cm) or 12 in. (30 cm) are suitable lengths. Sit comfortably in good light, in a chair without restricting armrests. Have the ball of yarn to your right. If possible, pull the end of the yarn out from the center of the ball, so that the ball does not roll around.

MAKING A SLIP KNOT

The very first step for almost everything one does in knitting is to make a slip knot on one needle.

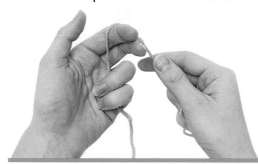

STEP 1
Pull a short length of yarn from the ball and hold the end in your left hand. Wind the yarn from the ball clockwise round the first and second fingers of this hand.

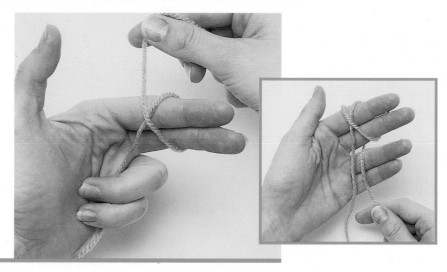

STEP 2
Wind the yarn round again, behind the first loop, so that the second loop is nearer the base of your fingers.

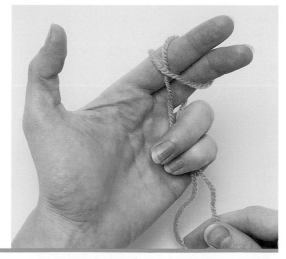

STEP 3
Hold both ends of the yarn under the third and fourth fingers of your left hand.

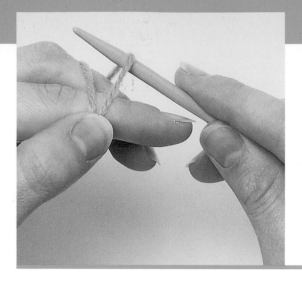

STEP 4
Take a knitting needle in your right hand and slip the tip under the first (front) loop of yarn.

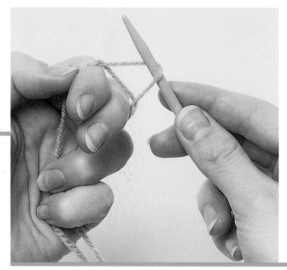

STEP 5
Catch the second (back) loop with the needle and pull it through the first loop, toward your fingertips.

STEP 6
Slip the loops of yarn off your fingers. Pull gently on the yarn and the yarn end to tighten the knot on the needle.

HOLDING YARN AND NEEDLES

There are several ways of holding the needles and yarn. For beginners the method shown below may seem complicated, but with practice it will result in a consistently even gauge and can be worked at speed.

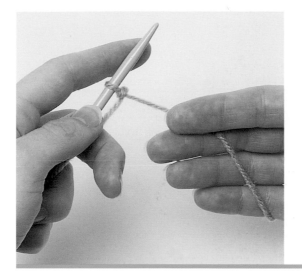

STEP 1
Hold the needle with the slip knot in your left hand, in the way you would hold a knife. To hold the yarn in your right hand, pass the little finger of your right hand over the yarn from the ball, then pass the forefinger of the same hand under the yarn from the ball, as shown. The yarn between the needle and your right hand should be slightly tensioned but not too tight.

STEP 2
The right forefinger is used to carry the yarn around the right needle tip. Hold both needles quite close to the tips. Rest the other end of the right needle against your body.

CASTING ON

Casting on creates a series of stitches on one needle that forms the edge of your knitting. There are several ways to cast on, each suitable for a different purpose. Some methods give a firm edge with little stretch; others form a more elastic edge suitable for beginning a garment piece with ribbing; yet others result in a loose edge suitable for lace stitches. The following two-needle (cable) cast-on forms a firm but elastic edge suitable for most purposes.

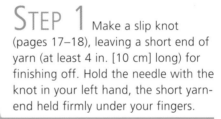

STEP 1 Make a slip knot (pages 17–18), leaving a short end of yarn (at least 4 in. [10 cm] long) for finishing off. Hold the needle with the knot in your left hand, the short yarn-end held firmly under your fingers.

STEP 2 Take the other needle in your right hand and insert the tip from left to right into the slip loop, beneath the left needle.

STEP 3
Holding the yarn from the ball in your right hand, pass it counterclockwise around (that is, behind) the tip of the right needle, then between the two needles from left to right.

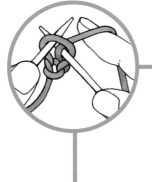

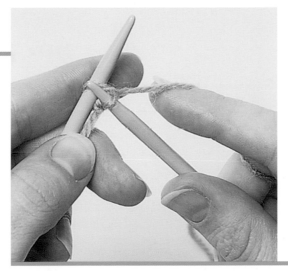

STEP 4
Use the right needle to draw the new loop of yarn through the previous loop, scooping from the back.

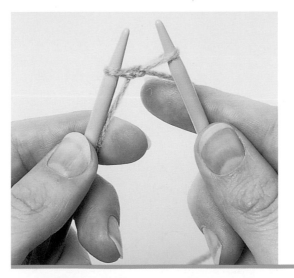

STEP 5
Bring the loop to the front of the work.

STEP 6 Insert the tip of the left needle into the new loop.

STEP 7 Pass the new loop onto the left needle.

TO MAKE A TIGHTER EDGE

Should a firmer edge be called for—when beginning a garment with garter stitch (pages 24–25), for example— work the two-needle cast-on as shown, then work the first row through the back loops of the stitches instead of the front, that is, inserting the right needle into each stitch from right to left (instead of left to right). This tightens the stitches by twisting them.

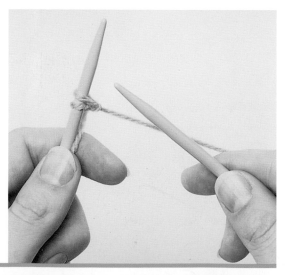

STEP 8 Tighten it gently into place (2 stitches made).

TO MAKE A LOOSER EDGE

Sometimes a looser or less bulky edge is required, when beginning a piece of lace knitting, for example, or where the edge will be sewn into a seam. To make a loose cast-on, work as shown, but for each new stitch insert the point of the right needle into the loop of the stitch just formed instead of behind it.

STEP 9 Insert the tip of the right needle under the left needle, behind the loop of the stitch just made.

STEP 10 As before, wind the yarn round the right needle, pull the new loop through and pass it to the left needle (three stitches made).

TIP
Don't worry if your cast-on stitches look a little uneven. When you work the first row of knitting, the yarn will tend to move around and balance them up. When the knitting is finished, you can gently stretch and release the edge to complete the process. Don't over-tighten your cast-on stitches onto the left needle. When you come to work the first row of knitting, the tip of the right needle should slip comfortably into the loop of each stitch. Experience will tell you how tight the stitches should be.

STEP 11 Repeat steps 9 and 10 until you have the number of stitches you need for a complete row.

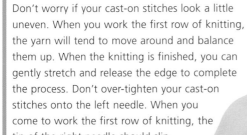

How to knit

The knit stitch is one of two fundamental stitches in knitting. To knit a stitch, you use the right needle to pull a loop of yarn toward you through the stitch on the left needle. To practice the knit stitch, begin first by casting on about 20 stitches (pages 20–23).

STEP 1 Hold the needle with the cast-on stitches in your left hand, with the first stitch about 1 in. (2.5 cm) from the tip. Take up the ball yarn in your right hand (page 19) and hold it together with the empty needle, held as you would a knife. Insert the tip of the right needle from left to right through the first stitch on the left needle, under the left needle and in front of the yarn held in your right hand.

STEP 2 With your right forefinger carry the yarn counterclockwise over the tip of the right needle and then between the two needles from left to right. Use the tip of the right needle to pull the loop of yarn forward through the first stitch on the left needle.

TIP

If your stitches look uneven, try the following:
1. Try to form the stitches close to the needle tips. The stitch you are knitting into on the left needle should be no more than ½–1 in. (1–2.5 cm) from the tip, depending on the needle size and yarn weight. The new stitch you make on the right needle should be at a similar distance from the tip of the right needle.
2. Take a close look at your last row of knit stitches (see illustration below). Follow the path of the yarn along the needle toward the point: each stitch loops from front right over the needle to back left, down through the loop of the stitch below and up through the loop of the next stitch along. Each stitch pushes the loop of the stitch below *away* from you as you knit.

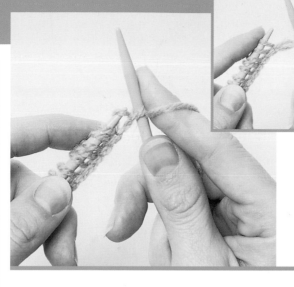

STEP 3 Slip the original stitch off the left needle. The newly made knit stitch is on the right needle. One knit stitch has been worked.

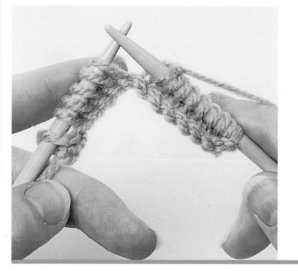

STEP 4 To knit a row, repeat steps 1–3. After every few stitches, push the stitches on the right needle away from the tip to prevent them bunching together and push the stitches on the left needle toward the tip to prevent stretching them. When all the stitches from the left needle have been worked onto the right needle, one row of knit stitches is complete.

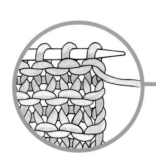

STEP 5 Turn the work around, holding the needle with the stitches in your left hand. Knit another row. Repeat this step several times. The resulting stitch pattern is called garter stitch, formed by knitting all the stitches on every row. Both sides of the worked piece have the same appearance.

How to Purl

The purl stitch is the second fundamental knitting stitch. To purl a stitch, you use the right needle to pull a loop of yarn away from you through the stitch on the left needle. The result is the same as a knit stitch with the wrong side facing you; a knit stitch made backward. To practice the purl stitch, begin first by casting on about 20 stitches (pages 20–23).

STEP 1 Hold the needle with the stitches on in your left hand, and the empty needle in your right hand together with the yarn. Hold the yarn in front of the right needle and insert the tip of the right needle into the first stitch on the left needle, from right to left, in front of the left needle.

STEP 2 Use your right forefinger to wrap the yarn counterclockwise around the right needle tip as shown.

TIP

Take a close look at your last row of purl stitches (see illustration, bottom). Follow the path of the yarn along the needle toward the point: each stitch loops from front right over the needle to back left, down through the loop of the stitch below and up through the loop of the next stitch along. Each new stitch pushes the loop of the stitch below *toward* you as you purl.

STEP 3 With the tip of the right needle, pull the loop of yarn back through the first stitch.

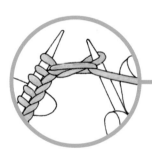

STEP 4 Slip the original stitch off the left needle. The newly made purl stitch is on the right needle. One purl stitch has been worked.

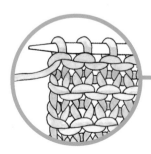

STEP 5

To purl a row, repeat steps 1–4 until all the stitches from the left needle have been worked onto the right needle. Notice how the purl row forms a row of purl bumps on the side of the work facing you. If you purl several rows, the appearance of the work will be the same as for garter stitch (where all the rows are made up of knit stitches).

STOCKINETTE STITCH

The stockinette stitch is the best-known combination of knit and purl. It is formed, very simply, by alternating one row of knit stitches with one row of purl stitches. It is the most widely used stitch in knitting as it forms a smooth, flexible fabric suitable for all kinds of garments. It requires less yarn than garter stitch and the length of an item knitted in stockinette increases more quickly because the rows are less tightly packed. When you work a knit row, the purl bumps of the stitches are formed at the back, that is, on the side facing away from you. When you work a purl row, the purl bumps are formed on the side facing you.

TIP

If your rows look uneven, with every other row of stitches consistently larger, this usually means you are purling more loosely than you are knitting (although it may be the other way round!). Try to keep the stitches you are working close to the needle tips, as described on page 25. Some knitters find it helpful to use a needle one size smaller for purl rows (if the purl rows are consistently looser). However it is better to try to improve your technique, without altering the needle size, if you can.

When you work alternate rows of knit and purl, one side of the work (the side facing you as you work a knit row) is quite smooth. This is the knit side, the right side of stockinette.

The other side (the side facing you as you work a purl row) shows all the purl bumps of every row. This is the purl side, the wrong side of stockinette.

REVERSE STOCKINETTE STITCH

The reverse stockinette stitch is simply stockinette stitch worked with the purl side as the right side of the work. It is often worked by beginning with a purl row.

BINDING OFF

Binding off is the most commonly used method of securing stitches on a finished piece of knitting. Binding off links stitches that are no longer required, to prevent them from unraveling. A bound-off edge may be worked across all the stitches at the end of a piece of knitting, or certain groups of stitches may be bound off in the course of the knitting in order to shape the work, for example at an armhole. A bound-off edge should not be too loose or too tight. It should stretch by about the same amount as the rest of the knitted piece. Sometimes a more elastic edge is required, for example on a neckband. To work a loose bind-off, change to a needle one or two sizes larger than the previous rows.

STEP 1 Knit the first two stitches on the left needle in the usual way onto the right needle. Insert the tip of the left needle, from left to right, through the front of the first stitch on the right needle (the stitch farthest right).

STEP 2 Lift the first stitch over the second stitch and off the right needle.

STEP 3 One stitch remains on the right needle. One stitch has been bound off.

STEP 4 Knit the next stitch. There are now two stitches on the right needle. Repeat steps 2–4 as many times as required. When binding off all stitches, you should end with one stitch on the right needle. Cut the yarn, leaving a tail of at least 6 in. (15 cm).

TIPS

1. When binding off a certain number of stitches, to shape a neck or armhole for example, always count the stitches as you lift them off, not as you knit them. The stitch remaining on the right needle does not count as a bound-off stitch—it becomes the first stitch of the next row.

2. When binding off a piece worked in rib or another textured stitch, keep the appearance consistent by working each stitch as knit or purl according to the stitch pattern.

3. When binding off purl stitches, keep the yarn at the front of the work. To lift off the right-hand stitch, insert the left needle into the back of this stitch, from left to right.

STEP 5 Wrap the tail around the right needle. Lift the last stitch on the right needle over the loop and pull the tail through the last stitch to make a neat finish. The tail may be run in later along a seam, or a longer tail may be left and used for sewing a seam.

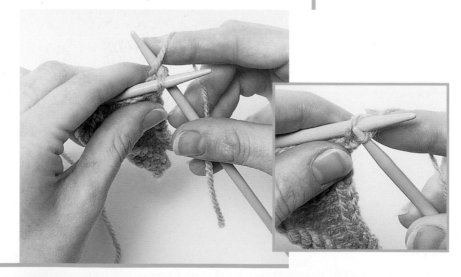

JOINING IN A NEW BALL

Use this technique to join in a new ball of yarn (when the previous ball is used up) or to join in another color when knitting in stripes. Always avoid joining in a new ball halfway through a row.

STEP 1 Tie the new yarn around the end of the old yarn, leaving a tail of at least 6 in. (15 cm).

TIP
One row usually requires a length of yarn approximately four times the width of the work (except for complicated stitch patterns). When you think you have enough yarn left for two rows, tie a slip knot at the center of the remaining length of yarn. Work one row. If you reach the knot, untie it and complete the row, then join in a new ball. If you don't reach the knot, untie it and repeat the process.

STEP 2 Push the knot up close to the edge of the work and begin the next row with the new ball. When the piece is complete, undo the knot and run in the yarn ends (page 45).

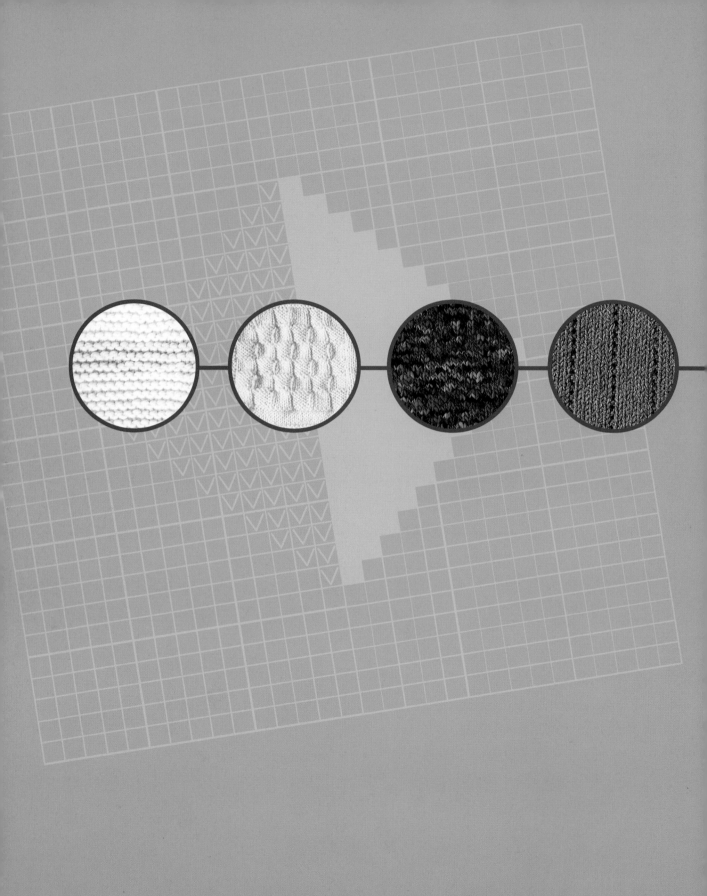

PROJECTS AND TECHNIQUES

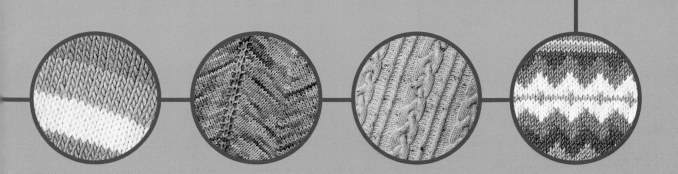

Now that you have learned the basic techniques of knitting, you can move on to the more advanced techniques described in this section. Subjects include assembling garments, working to correct gauge, working from knitting patterns, shaping your knitting, knitting in the round, adding details such as collars and buttonholes, different types of stitch patterns, Fair Isle (two-color) knitting, intarsia (picture) knitting, and adding finishing touches such as beads and pompoms.

Throughout this section you will also find beautiful and inspirational projects. These are arranged in order of the knowledge required to complete them, beginning with the simplest project (Striped Garter Scarf, pages 38–39) and ending with the most elaborate (Child's Sweater, pages 122–125). By working through this book page by page, you will find that each project puts only those skills and techniques you have learned into practice. Here is your chance to create something special for yourself or your family and friends—and to learn the skills for a lifetime's knitting.

COMBINING KNIT AND PURL

ROWS OF KNIT AND PURL STITCHES

One or more rows of reverse stockinette stitch on a background of stockinette stitch will produce a pronounced ridge across the width of the knitting. Simple combinations of knit and purl rows can therefore be used to make a variety of ridged patterns.

KNITTING ABBREVIATIONS

k—knit   **p**—purl

Asterisks or parentheses can be used to indicate the repetition of a sequence of stitches, e.g. *K2, p1, rep from * to end *means* knit two stitches, then purl one stitch then repeat this sequence to the end of the row.

For more information about knitting abbreviations and instructions, see Working from Patterns (pages 52–55). For a list of common knitting abbreviations, see page 127.

RIDGE STITCH SUITABLE FOR ANY NUMBER OF STITCHES.
Work 4 rows in stockinette stitch as follows:
Row 1 K.
Row 2 P.
Row 3 K.
Row 4 P.
Then work 4 rows in reverse stockinette stitch as follows:
Row 5 P.
Row 6 K.
Row 7 P.
Row 8 K.
Repeat these 8 rows.

RANDOM GARTER ROWS SUITABLE FOR ANY NUMBER OF STITCHES.
Work in stockinette stitch, but at random intervals replace a right-side (knit) row with a purl row.
Each reverse row forms a small ridge across the work. (Reverse rows may also be worked at regular intervals, if desired.)

KNIT AND PURL STITCHES IN THE SAME ROW

Vertical ribs and other textures are made by working knit and purl stitches in the same row.

PATTERN REPEATS AND STITCH MULTIPLES

Always work on the correct number of stitches when working any stitch pattern or the pattern sequence will be lost. In the examples on pages 36–37, each pattern gives a requirement for the number of stitches, for example "requires a multiple of 3 sts" means this pattern must be worked on a number of stitches that divides exactly by 3 (such as 24, 33, or 99). The pattern repeat is 3 sts. "requires a multiple of 4 sts, plus 1" means this pattern must be worked on a number of stitches that is a multiple of 4 (such as 24, 36, or 100) plus one extra stitch (making 25, 37, or 101). Such a pattern repeats over 4 sts and one extra stitch is required to make it symmetrical.

YARN POSITION

When working these stitch patterns, it is necessary to pass the yarn correctly between the needles into the position required for a purl stitch following a knit stitch, and vice versa.

After a knit stitch and before a purl stitch, bring the yarn to the front of the work between the needles, ready to purl the next stitch.

After a purl stitch and before a knit stitch, take the yarn to the back of the work between the needles, ready to knit the next stitch.

RIB PATTERNS

In these patterns, stitches are arranged in alternate vertical lines—one line with the smooth (knit) side of the stitches to the front, and the next line with the purl bump (purl) side of the stitches to the front. The effect is an elastic fabric that stretches easily widthwise and does not curl, making it suitable for lower edges, cuffs, neckbands, and other borders. Such details are usually worked on needles two sizes smaller than those used for the main sections. Even when used for the main parts of garments, rib patterns often require smaller needles to allow them to look neat.

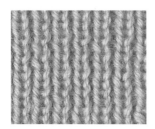

K1, P1 RIB REQUIRES AN EVEN NUMBER OF STITCHES
Row 1 *K1, p1, repeat from * to end.
Repeat this row.

K2, P2 RIB REQUIRES A MULTIPLE OF 4 STITCHES
Row 1 *K2, p2, repeat from * to end.
Repeat this row.

K1, P2 RIB REQUIRES A MULTIPLE OF 3 STITCHES
Note that this rib has a different appearance on each side.
Row 1 P1, *k1, p2, repeat from * to last 2 sts, k1, p1.
Row 2 K1, *p1, k2, repeat from * to last 2 sts, p1, k1.
Repeat these 2 rows.

BROKEN RIB REQUIRES A MULTIPLE OF 4 STITCHES, PLUS 1
This stitch is not quite so elastic as a true rib, because some of the vertical lines are broken by being worked as knit stitches on every row. It will lie flat without curling.
Row 1 K2, *p1, k3, repeat from * to last 3 sts, p1, k2.
Row 2 *P1, k3, repeat from * to last st, p1.
Repeat these 2 rows.

SEED STITCHES

In these stitch patterns, reverse stitches (purl stitches on right-side rows or knit stitches on wrong-side rows) are arranged alternately along each row and also vertically, making firm flat fabrics suitable for borders and edgings, but with little elasticity.

SEED STITCH REQUIRES AN ODD NUMBER OF STITCHES
Row 1 *K1, p1, repeat from * to last st, k1. Repeat this row. Note how each stitch is reversed on the second row, because of the odd number of stitches.

MOSS STITCH REQUIRES AN ODD NUMBER OF STITCHES
Row 1 *K1, p1, repeat from * to last st, k1.
Row 2 *P1, k1, repeat from * to last st, p1.
Row 3 *P1, k1, repeat from * to last st, p1.
Row 4 *K1, p1, repeat from * to last st, k1.
Repeat these 4 rows.

REVERSED STITCH PATTERNS

These patterns utilize the textural effect of stitches worked in reverse on a stockinette stitch background.

CATERPILLAR STITCH REQUIRES A MULTIPLE OF 8 STS, PLUS 2
Row 1 *K2, p6, repeat from * to last 2 sts, k2.
Row 2 P.
Row 3 K.
Row 4 P.
Row 5 P4, *k2, p6, repeat from * to last 6 sts, k2, p4.
Rows 6–8 Repeat rows 2–4.
Repeat these 8 rows.

LITTLE SQUARES REQUIRES A MULTIPLE OF 6 STS, PLUS 3
Row 1 *K3, p3, repeat from * to last 3 sts, k3.
Row 2 *P3, k3, repeat from * to last 3 sts, p3.
Row 3 Repeat row 1.
Row 4 Repeat row 2.
Row 5 *P3, k3, repeat from * to last 3 sts, p3.
Row 6 *K3, p3, repeat from * to last 3 sts, k3.
Row 7 Repeat row 5.
Row 8 Repeat row 6.
Repeat these 8 rows.

PROJECT 1
STRIPED GARTER SCARF

Make this scarf in your own choice of colors: worked
on large needles in the simplest of stitches, it's an ideal
project for a beginner. Practice achieving an even gauge,
but don't worry too much; as you wear it and wash it,
uneven stitches will tend to disappear!

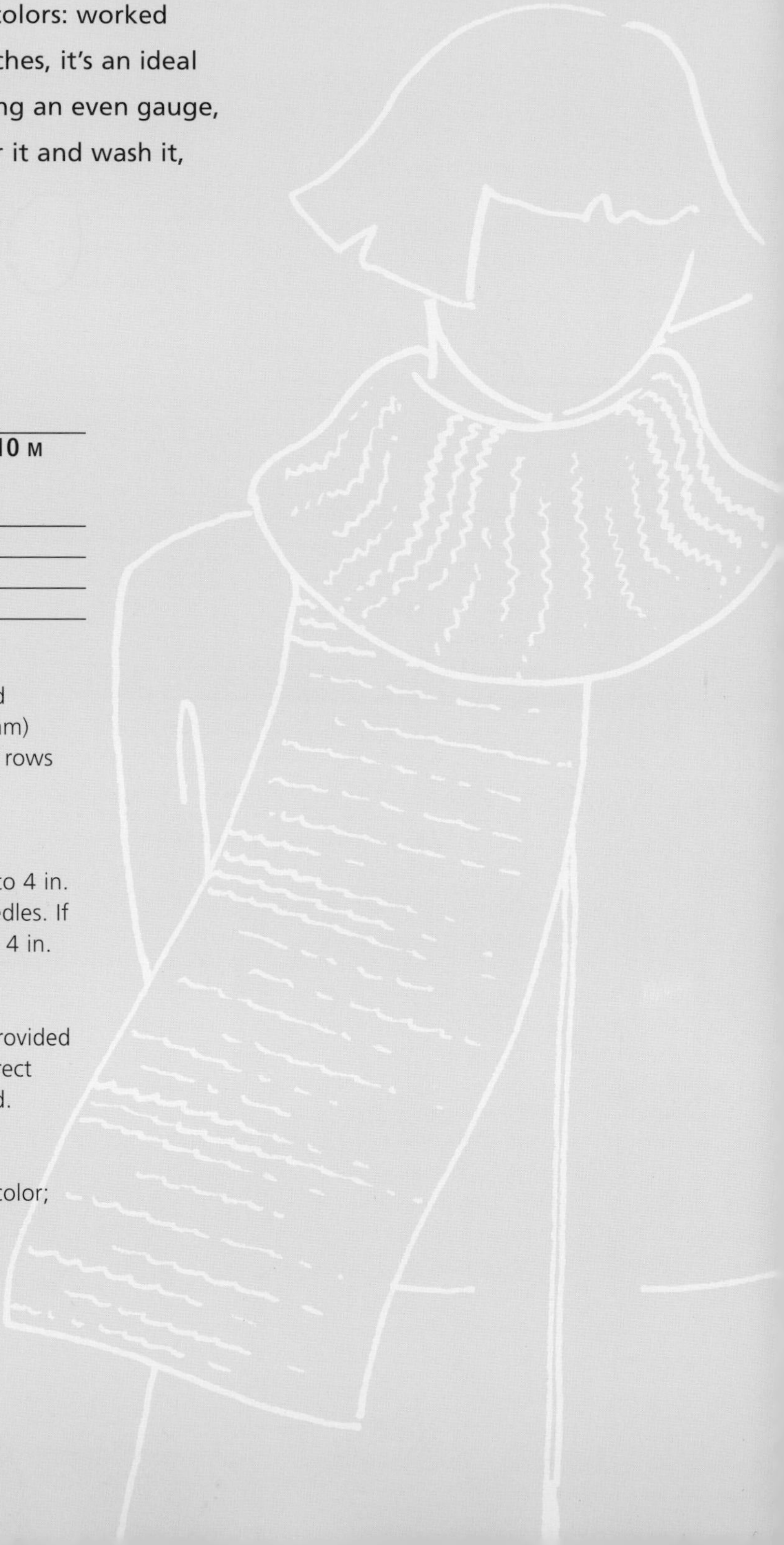

FINISHED SIZE
9 x 61 in. (23 x 155 cm)

MATERIALS
KING COLE MAGNUM CHUNKY (APPROX. 120 YDS/110 M
PER 100 G BALL)

COLOR A avocado (shade 173) 1 100-g ball

COLOR B blossom (shade 177) 1

COLOR C butter (shade 126) 1

NEEDLES size 10½ (6½ mm)

GAUGE
Required gauge over garter stitch is 12 sts and
20 rows to 4 in. (10 cm).Using size 10½ (6½ mm)
needles and col.A cast on 14 sts and work 24 rows
garter stitch (all rows knit). Measure gauge
(pages 50–51).

 If your gauge is tight, with more sts or rows to 4 in.
(10 cm), try another test-piece with larger needles. If
your gauge is loose, with fewer sts or rows to 4 in.
(10 cm), try again with smaller needles.

Note that for this scarf, gauge is not crucial provided
a change in size is acceptable, although incorrect
gauge may affect the amount of yarn required.

ABBREVIATIONS
k—knit; rep—repeat; st(s)—stitch(es); col.—color;
in.—inches; cm—centimeters.

SCARF

Using size 10½ (6½ mm) needles and col.A cast on 27 sts.

* Using col.A, k 20 rows. 20 rows garter stitch made.

Note how these rows form 10 ridges on the front of the work and 10 ridges on the back.

Change to col.B. K 6 rows

Change to col.C. K 20 rows.

Change to col.A. K 6 rows.

Change to col.B. K 20 rows.

Change to col.C. K 6 rows. * 78 rows garter st.

Rep from * to * twice more.

Rep first 72 rows once more, thus ending 20 rows col.B.

Bind off with col.B.

TO FINISH

Run in all the yarn ends down the side edges of the scarf.

This stitch should not be pressed. If required, block to size using water-spray method (page 41).

TIPS

1. Remember, when you have knitted an *even* number of rows, the cast-on tail of yarn will be on the left of the work as you begin the next row.
2. When changing colors, cut the old color leaving a 6 in. (15 cm) tail and tie the new color round it, leaving another 6 in. (15 cm) tail (page 31).

FINISHING

BLOCKING

The secret of a neatly finished garment is to "block" the pieces before joining them together. This process evens out the gauge in the finished work by relaxing the stitches and fixing their size and shape. It also helps edges to lie flat without curling.

Always refer to the ball-bands of the yarns you have used; some novelty yarns, including lurex, should never be blocked or pressed. Yarns that require minimum pressing are best blocked using the wet-spray method; these include long-haired yarns, synthetics, and synthetic blends.

Natural fiber yarns may usually be blocked with warm steam, either using a warm iron and a damp pressing cloth or a steam iron and a dry cloth. If your garment includes a combination of yarns, use the option suited to the most delicate yarn. Textured stitches should be treated with caution as over-pressing can permanently change their appearance. Only block a ribbed fabric if you want to change its appearance and behavior permanently by stretching it.

The knitting must be pinned out flat and square, and for this you will need a suitable surface. An ironing board is sufficient for small knitted pieces. Larger pieces obviously require a larger surface—about 36 in. (90 cm) square is a useful size. You will also need a good supply of large-headed rustproof pins. Glass-headed pins or T-pins are ideal.

TIPS

1. Use your gauge test-piece to try out the process you consider best suited to your work. If in doubt, use the wet-spray method.
2. To make your own blocking board, cover a piece of flat board with a layer of quilter's batting and an overlayer of cotton fabric, both smoothly stretched over the edges and attached firmly at the back with a glue gun or staples. The fabric should be made of cotton or similar material, to withstand the heat of the iron, and a check pattern is a good aid to pinning out the pieces with the edges straight.

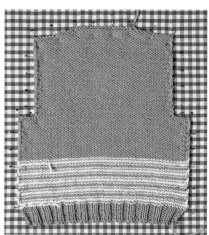

Lay the knitting right side down on the blocking board (see right) and pin it to shape, using the check pattern as a guide to keep unshaped edges straight. Check the measurements against the pattern instructions. Depending on the yarn, you may be able to ease or stretch the piece if necessary, but only by a small amount. Use lots of large-headed pins inserted at right angles to the edges, sliding them sideways into the layers to hold the edges flat without curling. Ribbing that is intended to gather in the edge of a garment should not be pinned. Leave it free as shown here. The two main methods of blocking—the warm-steam and wet-spray methods—are described on the opposite page. Choose the method most appropriate to the yarn(s) you have used.

WARM-STEAM METHOD

Never use an iron directly on a knitted surface. Use a warm iron and a damp pressing cloth or a steam iron and a dry cloth. The cloth should be made of cotton, and a damp cloth should be thoroughly wetted then well wrung out. Heat the iron to the setting recommended on the ball-band and lay the cloth over the knitting. Do not press down or move the iron over the cloth. Instead, hold the iron lightly on the surface for a few seconds, then lift and replace it until all the surface has been steamed. Remember, ribbing should never be pressed unless you want to reduce its elasticity. Leave the work pinned to the board, with the board flat, until the knitting is completely dry.

WET-SPRAY METHOD

Use a spray bottle to dampen the work thoroughly, patting it gently with your hand to help the moisture penetrate the fibers. Leave the work pinned to the board, with the board flat, until the knitting is completely dry.

SEAMS

How you sew together (or "seam") the various parts of your knitted piece has a great effect on final appearance. Knitting produces a flexible, comfortable fabric that can be spoiled by tight or lumpy seams. However, firm seams in certain places, such as shoulder seams, can help a garment retain its shape.

Always use a blunt-tipped needle, such as a tapestry needle, for sewing seams. Never use a needle with a sharp point. Your stitches should not split the knitted yarn but pass between the strands. Blunt-tipped needles are available in several sizes to suit different thicknesses of yarn. When joining matching edges, such as side or shoulder seams, the number of rows or stitches on each side should be the same, so it is not always necessary to use pins. Seams joining stitches to rows should be pinned with large-headed pins at right angles to the edges, or if you prefer you can use small safety pins.

To thread the needle, fold the end of the yarn over, hold it close to the loop, and push the loop through the eye of the needle. Never finish by breaking the yarn—always use scissors to cut it.

MATTRESS STITCH

The mattress stitch is used to join the side edges of two pieces that have the same number of rows. The ends of the rows are matched together exactly for a neat finish. This seam is usually worked one whole stitch in from each vertical edge. If the knitting includes a selvage stitch (page 59) at each side, these will provide a useful guide to placing the needle and will be concealed in the finished seam.

(page 59)

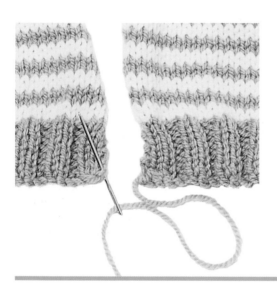

STEP 1
Begin at the lower edge of the work with a figure eight. Lay both pieces flat with the right sides uppermost and thread the tail of yarn from the casting on into the needle. Bring the needle up from the wrong side to the right side, one stitch in from the corner of the piece without the tail, as shown.

STEP 2
Next, bring the needle up from the wrong side to the right side of the corresponding position on the piece with the tail, completing the figure eight. Pull gently to tighten.

STEP 3 Insert the needle between the first and second stitches of the first row of the piece without the tail, bring it out again between the first and second stitches, one row along the edge, thus catching one strand of yarn on the needle.

STEP 4 On the opposite side of the seam (the piece with the tail), insert the needle between the first and second stitches of the first row and bring it out again between the first and second stitches, two rows along the edge, thus catching two strands of yarn on the needle.

STEP 5 On the opposite side of the seam, insert the needle where it last emerged; bring it out again two rows higher, thus catching two strands of yarn on the needle. Pull the thread to close the gap. The seam should not be shorter than the rest of the garment. Repeat step 5 to the top of the seam. Take the needle through to the wrong side and run in the yarn end along the seam (page 45).

SEAMING A SIDE EDGE TO A BOUND-OFF EDGE

To join the top edge of a sleeve to an armhole edge, the last row of stitches on the sleeve must be sewn to the row ends of the armhole. It is often advisable to pin such a seam as the number of stitches will rarely correspond with the number of rows.

TIP

When working backstitch, keep the needle vertical to the surface of the work when pushing it in and out to avoid splitting stitches. The stitches of the seam should be placed through the centers of the knitted stitches.

STEP 1 The stitching is worked in yellow to show the path of the yarn. Bring the needle up at the center of the first stitch of the bound-off edge. Insert the needle between the first and second stitches of the row opposite and bring it out again two rows along this edge, thus catching two strands of yarn on the needle.

STEP 2 Re-insert the needle at the center of the same stitch of the bound-off edge and bring it up again at the center of the next stitch along. Pull gently to close the gap. Repeat steps 1 and 2. Depending on the number of stitches and rows you are joining, you will probably, at regular intervals, need to pick up just one strand from the row-end side of the seam, instead of two strands. Spread these smaller stitches evenly to avoid a puckered seam.

BACKSTITCH SEAM

This is a strong seam used where firmness is required, for example on a shoulder seam.

STEP 1 Again, the sewing is shown here in yellow for clarity. Lay the pieces flat, the right sides facing together, and the edges matching. If necessary, pin the seam with pins at right angles to the edges as shown. Bring the needle up between the first and second stitches of both pieces, leaving a 6 in. (15 cm) tail at the back. Take the needle around the side edge and up through the same place to secure the yarn. Take the needle around the side edge again and bring it up through both layers, one whole stitch along from the previous position.

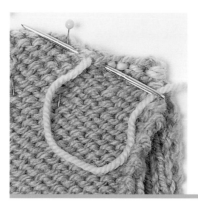

TIP

Where a new ball or color is joined in, there will be two tails to run in. Unpick the knot that joins them and run one end up the seam and the other down, to avoid a lump.

$\text{STEP } 2$ Insert the needle at the end of the previous backstitch and bring it out again one whole knitted stitch along the edge from where it last emerged. Repeat step 2. When the seam is complete, run in both the yarn end (see below) and the starting tail.

YARN ENDS

All pieces of knitting begin and end with a tail of yarn, and more are created when you join in a new ball, change colors, and sew up seams.

Always make these tails at least 6 in. (15 cm) long, so that they can be threaded into a needle easily and run in as below. Never knot the tails and cut them off short; knots can work loose and the adjacent stitches will unravel. With a little planning, you can leave longer ends where they will be useful to join seams, so avoiding joining in extra lengths for sewing up.

RUN IN ALONG A SEAM

Most yarn ends may be run in along the wrong side of a seam.

Thread the tail into a blunt-tipped tapestry needle. Run the needle in and out of the edge stitches along the wrong side of the seam for at least 2 in. (5 cm). Pull the needle through and cut off excess yarn.

RUN IN ALONG A ROW

Where a design requires many color changes, all those yarn tails can make the seams very bulky. For a neat finish, run in the ends before blocking and sewing up.

Unpick any knots joining the colors together. Thread each tail in turn into a blunt-tipped knitters' tapestry needle and weave it in and out of the purl bumps of a row of the same color on the wrong side of the work, for at least 2 in. (5 cm). Pull the needle through but do not over-tighten. Check that the run-in end does not show on the right side. Cut off the excess yarn.

PICKING UP STITCHES

The "pick up and knit" technique is used to begin a neckband or border directly from the edge of a piece of knitting, avoiding the need to cast on a separate piece and join it with a seam. The row of stitches formed in this way is more elastic and less bulky than a seam and is ideal for neckbands and armhole borders.

You will already have completed the main piece(s), so you start with a fresh yarn end, leaving at least 4 in. (10 cm) to be run in later. Work the first row as below, count the stitches again, and then complete the neckband or border according to your pattern. Whatever stitch you use for the border, always work the picked-up stitches as knit stitches, usually with the right side of the work facing you.

SPACING EVENLY

To ensure the picked-up stitches are evenly spaced, lay the work on a flat surface, measure the edge, and divide it into a convenient number of sections of around 2–3 in. (5–7.5 cm), to suit the length of the edge and the number of stitches required. Mark these sections with pins or markers (see right). Now divide the number of stitches required by the number of sections and pick up the resulting number of stitches from each section of the edge.

TIP

For very bulky yarns, it may be preferable to insert the needle tip in the center of the first stitch of the row, i.e. under only one thread. This makes a less bulky join, but with finer yarns tends to look uneven.

TO PICK UP ALONG A SIDE EDGE OF KNITTING

The number of stitches required will usually be less than the number of rows along the edge, so stitches will not be picked up from all rows. Mark the spacing as above and try to spread the stitches evenly.

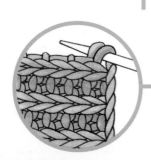

STEP 1 Hold the piece right-side up and work from right to left along the edge. Take a needle of the size specified in your pattern and insert its tip from front to back between the first two stitches of the first row, i.e. one whole stitch in from the edge.

STEP 2
Hold the yarn in your right hand and the edge of the main piece between your left thumb and forefinger, close to the needle. Wind the yarn around the tip of the needle.

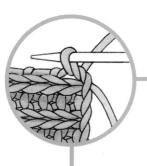

STEP 3
Draw it through in the same way as you would knit a stitch. A new stitch is formed on the needle.

STEP 4
Repeat steps 1–3 along the edge, picking up the correct number of stitches between each pair of markers, until you have the required number of stitches on the needle.

BABY AFGHAN

Three different stitch patterns, worked in strips, form a textured patchwork that is great fun to knit. Each pattern square is worked over the same number of stitches and rows but the gauges differ slightly, adding interest to the surface.

FINISHED SIZE
26 x 30 in. (66 x 76 cm)

MATERIALS
PATONS DIPLOMA GOLD ARAN (APPROX. 180 YDS/164 M PER 100 G BALL)

COLOR cream (shade 8121) 4 100-g balls

NEEDLES sizes 7 (4½ mm) and 4 (3½ mm)

GAUGE
Required gauge over stockinette is 19 sts and 25 rows to 4 in. (10 cm). Using size 7 (4½ mm) needles, cast on 21 sts and work 28 rows stockinette. Measure gauge (pages 50–51).

If your gauge is tight, with more sts or rows to 4 in. (10 cm), try another test-piece with larger needles. If your gauge is loose, with fewer sts or rows to 4 in. (10 cm), try again with smaller needles. If your gauge is correct, the gauge over each pattern should also be correct.

NOTES
1. Make this afghan any size you wish. To make the strips longer, simply repeat the pattern squares in order. To increase the width, make more strips. Allow 100 g of yarn for every 5 squares; for a large afghan you may require extra yarn for the border.

2. For this afghan, gauge is not crucial provided a change in size is acceptable, although incorrect gauge may affect the amount of yarn required.

3. Each strip is worked with one selvage stitch (page 59) at each edge as described in these instructions.

ABBREVIATIONS
k—knit; **p**—purl; **rep**—repeat; **st(s)**—stitch(es); **in.**—inches; **cm**—centimeters.

FIRST STRIP
Using size 7 (4½ mm) needles cast on 32 sts.

PATTERN SQUARE A garter stripes

Row 1 K.

Row 2 K1, p to last st, k1.

Rep these 2 rows twice more. (6 rows stockinette made.)

Row 7 K.

Rep this row 3 more times. (4 rows garter st made.) 10 rows in all.

Rep these 10 rows twice more. 30 rows.

Work rows 1–6 again. 36 rows.

Break Line: K 2 rows.

PATTERN SQUARE B checkers

Row 1 K1, *p5, k5, rep from * to last st, kl.

Rep this row 5 more times. 6 rows.

Row 7 K1, *k5, p5, rep from * to last st, k1.

Rep this row 5 more times. 12 rows.

Rep these 12 rows twice more. 36 rows.

Work 2 rows Break Line as above.

PATTERN SQUARE C little posts

Row 1 K.

Row 2 K1, p to last st, k1.

Rep these 2 rows once more. 4 rows.

Row 5 K3, *p2, k6, rep from * to last 5 sts, p2, k3.

Row 6 K1, p2, *k2, p6, rep from * to last 5 sts, k2, p2, k1.

Rep these 2 rows 3 more times. 12 rows.

Row 13 K.

Row 14 K1, p to last st, k1.

Row 15 K7, *p2, k6, rep from * to last st, k1.

Row 16 K1, p6, *k2, p6, rep from * to last st, kl.

Rep rows 15 and 16, 3 more times. 22 rows.

Row 23 K.

Row 24 K1, p to last st, k1.

Rows 25–32 Work as rows 5–12.

Rows 33–36 Work as rows 1–4. 36 rows.

Work 2 rows Break Line as above.

Work 36 rows Pattern Square A, 2 rows Break Line, 36 rows Pattern Square B.

Bind off.

SECOND STRIP

Cast on 32 sts as for First Strip.

Work 36 rows Pattern Square B, 2 rows Break Line,
36 rows Pattern Square C, 2 rows Break Line,
36 rows Pattern Square A, 2 rows Break Line,
36 rows Pattern Square B, 2 rows Break Line,
36 rows Pattern Square C.

Bind off.

THIRD STRIP

Cast on 32 sts as for First Strip.

Work 36 rows Pattern Square C, 2 rows Break Line,
36 rows Pattern Square A, 2 rows Break Line,
36 rows Pattern Square B, 2 rows Break Line,
36 rows Pattern Square C, 2 rows Break Line,
36 rows Pattern Square A.

Bind off.

FOURTH STRIP

Work as First Strip.

ASSEMBLY

These stitch patterns should not be heavily pressed. Block strips using wet-spray method (page 41).

Join strips side by side in order as diagram, using mattress stitch (pages 42–43). Make sure you have all the cast-on edges at one end. Press seams lightly with a cool iron.

TOP BORDER

With right side of work facing, using size 4 (3½ mm) needles, pick up and k 122 sts from bound-off edges of joined strips, as follows:

31 sts from top edge of fourth strip, leave 2

selvage sts at seam, 30 sts from top edge of third strip, leave 2 selvage sts at seam, 30 sts from top edge of second strip, leave 2 selvage sts at seam, 31 sts from top edge of first strip. 122 sts in all.

K 5 rows, thus ending wrong-side row.

Bind off.

LOWER BORDER

Work to match Top Border, picking up sts from cast-on edges of strips.

SIDE BORDERS (MAKE 2)

With right side of work facing, using size 4 (3½ mm) needles, pick up and k 4 sts from side edge of border, then 3 sts from every 4 rows along side edge, ending with 4 sts from side edge of second border.

K 5 rows, thus ending wrong-side row.

Bind off.

Run in all the yarn ends on wrong side of seams (page 45). If required, block again using the wet-spray method (page 41).

first strip	second strip	third strip	fourth strip
B	C	A	B
A	B	C	A
C	A	B	C
B	C	A	B
A	B	C	A

ASSEMBLY DIAGRAM

GAUGE

Correct gauge is the key to knitting pieces to the correct size. The gauge of a knitted piece is a measure of the actual size of the knitted stitches, expressed as the number of stitches to a given width and the number of rows to a given length.

Most knitting pattern instructions include a recommended gauge and it is vital that you match this gauge exactly, otherwise, your work will be the wrong size. A recommended gauge on a ball-band or in a pattern instruction is chosen to give a correct "handle" to the work—too tight and the work will be stiff and heavy, too loose and it will tend to drop out of shape. So even if you compensate for incorrect gauge by working more or less rows or stitches, you may still be disappointed with the result.

FACTORS AFFECTING GAUGE

Gauge is affected by the type of yarn used, the size of the needles, the individual knitter, and the stitch pattern, and is crucial to the success of your work.

YARN USED Two knitted pieces in different weights of yarn, with the same number of stitches and rows, and on the same size needles, will differ in size. Always try to obtain the exact yarn quoted in the pattern instructions. Yarns with the same general description, e.g., "worsted," may differ slightly in weight from one manufacturer, or one fiber content, to another.

NEEDLE SIZE Two knitted pieces in exactly the same yarn, with the same number of stitches and rows, but done on different-size needles, will also differ in size. The larger the needles, the larger the individual stitches will be. Even the types of needles used can affect gauge. Different yarn fibers slip with varying degrees of ease over needle surfaces of plastic, wood, or steel. Always use the same pair of needles for the gauge test-piece as for the final knitted piece.

THE INDIVIDUAL KNITTER How you hold the yarn and needles in your hands also affects the gauge. Some knitters find that they need consistently larger or smaller needles

than stated in the pattern to obtain a correct gauge.

STITCH PATTERN Two knitted pieces made with exactly the same yarn, the same number of stitches and rows, and on the same-size needles will differ in size if the stitch pattern used is different. Some stitch patterns shrink or stretch the knitting sideways and some shrink or stretch it lengthwise. The block stitch shown below has several more rows to 4 in. (10 cm) than an equivalent piece of stockinette stitch.

MEASURING GAUGE

Before beginning any new project, knit
a test-piece in the following way

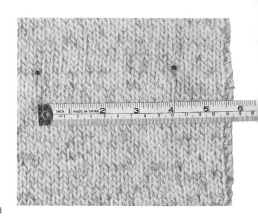

1. Read the pattern instructions to find the recommended gauge. This will usually be quoted as "x stitches and y rows to 4 in. (10 cm)" measured over a certain stitch pattern and using a certain size of needles.

2. Using the yarn that you intend to use for your knitted piece, and the needle size specified, cast on a few more stitches than the figure quoted, enough to make the test-piece about 6 in. (15 cm) wide. If you are working a particular stitch pattern, choose a number to suit the stitch repeat. Work in the required stitch pattern for about 6 in. (15 cm) and bind off. Block this test-piece (pages 40–41) in the way you intend to block the finished piece.

3. Lay the test-piece right side up on a flat surface and use a ruler or tape measure to insert two pins exactly 4 in. (10 cm) apart, at the center of the piece, along a straight row of stitches (see above). Make a note of the number of stitches between the pins, including any half stitches. This is the number of stitches to 4 in. (10 cm).

4. In the same way, measure off 4 in. (10 cm) vertically, inserting two pins exactly 4 in. (10 cm) apart at the center of the piece, along a straight line of stitches. Make a note of the number of rows between the pins, including any half rows. This is the number of rows to 4 in. (10 cm). Depending on the yarn and stitch pattern, it may be easier to turn the test-piece over and measure the rows on the reverse side. If your gauge matches the recommended gauge exactly, congratulations! If not, you must adjust your gauge as described below.

ADJUSTING GAUGE

If your test-piece has too many stitches or rows to 4 in. (10 cm), your work is too tight and you must work another test-piece using larger needles. If your test-piece has too few stitches or rows to 4 in. (10 cm), your work is too loose and you should work another test-piece using smaller needles. Block or press the new test-piece as before and measure the gauge as above. Repeat this process until your gauge is exactly right. Remember that a difference of one stitch or row over 4 in. (10 cm) can translate into a difference of 3 or 4 in. (7.5 or 10 cm) over the width or length of a complete garment so it is most important that you get the gauge right.

SUBSTITUTING YARNS

Sometimes it is impossible to find the exact yarn specified in pattern instructions, because manufacturers discontinue lines and colors for various reasons. Read the pattern instructions carefully and make a note of the recommended gauge and needle size, the yarn's fiber content, and the yardage, if quoted. If necessary, try to find another yarn to match all these criteria as closely as possible, the most important factor being the gauge. If possible, buy just one ball and make one or more test-pieces, matching the gauge before purchasing the bulk of the yarn. If the substitute yarn quotes a shorter yardage on the ball-band than the recommended yarn, extra yarn will be required. As a rule, cotton and cotton-blend yarns are particularly heavy and therefore have a shorter yardage.

WORKING FROM PATTERNS

At first glance, knitting instructions can appear daunting. However, far from being difficult to understand, most knitting instructions present information in a logical order, use similar terms and abbreviations, and are intended to be simple to follow, much like a cooking recipe. Always read a pattern through before you begin knitting, to ensure that you understand all the terms and abbreviations used and how the garment will be constructed.

It is also a good idea to keep a notebook in which to record your projects and sizing and body measurements for yourself and your family. Keep one of the ball bands from each yarn you use, as a reference for washing and pressing instructions, and also for recommended gauges. You can also keep a strand of each yarn for future reference.

When you check your gauge for a project, record the yarn, stitch, and needles you used to obtain the given gauge. Keep your gauge test-pieces too, either in the notebook or separately. For each project, make a note of anything in a pattern that you will need to repeat later for a matching piece, for example the number of rows on a sleeve. Take photographs of your finished projects and paste those in too. Your notebook will be an invaluable source of information in the future.

SIZING

Garment patterns usually include instructions for a range of sizes, with the measurements provided at the beginning, for example:

SIZING					
to fit bust/chest	32	34	36	38	in.
	81	86	92	97	cm
actual measurement	36	38	40	42	in.
	92	97	102	107	cm
length	20	22	23	23½	in.
	50.5	56	58.5	59.5	cm
sleeve length	16	17	17½	18	in.
	40.5	43	44.5	46	cm

Decide which system of measurement you intend to use, imperial (inches) or metric (centimeters). Although 4 in. are approximately equal to 10 cm, longer measurements multiply the inaccuracy: 40 in. measure close to 102 cm. So choose one system and stick to it throughout the project.

To fit bust/chest This is the body measurement, taken with a tape measure fitted snugly around the widest part of the bust or chest.

Actual measurement This is the actual measurement of the finished garment, which often includes several inches of "ease." In the table opposite, 4 in. (10 cm) of ease have been added to each bust/chest measurement. The ease allowance may be anything from 1 in. (2.5 cm) to 6 in. (15 cm) or more, depending on the style of garment and the fit required. The actual measurement is the width of the back plus the width of the front. In the case of garments such as cardigans, it is measured with the fastenings closed.

Length This measurement is usually taken from the top of the shoulder to the lower edge of the garment. Drop a tape measure from the top of the shoulder to find how long the garment will be on the body. Depending on the design, the length may sometimes be measured at the center back neck.

TIP

Keep a note of your own body measurements, but also check the measurements of your favorite garment by laying it out on a flat surface and measuring the width, length, and sleeve length. Remember the actual chest measurement is twice the width. Keep a note of these measurements to help you choose the correct size from a pattern.

Sleeve length This length is usually measured vertically through the center of the sleeve, not along the sloping, shaped edges. It is the length from the lower edge to the last row before shaping begins for the top of the sleeve, at the level of the underarm. In the case of oversize garments with deep armholes, the sleeve length may be considerably shorter than the body measurement from wrist to underarm. Many patterns include an adjustable sleeve length. Just before shaping begins for the top of the sleeve, there is a point where rows may be added or subtracted.

Other measurements These may also be included depending on the design of the garment.

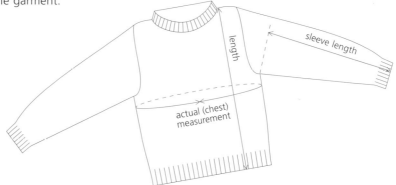

TIP

Before you start working from a pattern, highlight all the figures in a pattern that apply to your chosen size.

Decide which size you wish to make from the table of measurements provided with the instructions. Different sizes are given within the text of a pattern as 1st size (the smallest), followed by the larger sizes in brackets, and ending with the largest size thus: 1st size[2nd size, 3rd size, 4th size]. This format is repeated throughout a pattern for all the sets of figures that differ from one size to the next, for example the number of stitches to cast on, the number of rows to work, the number of increases, or the length to work to in inches (cm). Where only one figure is given, this applies to all sizes.

MATERIALS

Pattern instructions list the amounts of yarn required for each size, recommended needles sizes, and other requirements, such as stitch holders, buttons, and so on.

Always try to purchase the recommended yarn. If this is impossible, see Substituting Yarns (page 51). If possible, purchase all the yarn required for the project at the same time. If you try to purchase more yarn at a later date you may find the dye lots differ (page 13) and your project will be spoiled.

GAUGE

It is vital that you check your own gauge carefully (pages 50–51). The recommended gauge for any project will be quoted in the pattern.

ABBREVIATIONS

All the abbreviations used within a pattern are usually listed in alphabetical order together with their meaning. Abbreviations may vary slightly from one pattern source to the next, so read them carefully and make sure you understand them.

Note that different pattern producers may use either capital or lower case letters for abbreviations. The most commonly used knitting abbreviations are listed on page 127.

PARENTHESES AND ASTERISKS

Parentheses are sometimes used to indicate the repetition of a sequence of stitches. For example, "(K2tog, k1) 3 times" means "K2tog, k1, k2tog, k1, k2tog, k1."

Asterisks may be used for the same purpose. For example, "*K2tog, k1, rep from * twice more" *also* means "K2tog, k1, k2tog, k1, k2tog, k1."

Asterisks are also used to avoid repeating lengthy sections of instructions. For example, halfway through the instructions for the back of a sweater, you may find one (*) or two (**) asterisks with no apparent purpose. When you work the front, you will find instructions such as "work as Back to *" or perhaps "complete as Back from ** to end."

Asterisks and parentheses may also be used in combination. For example, "*K2, p1, (k1, p1) 3 times, rep from * to end." This means "K2, p1, k1, p1, k1, p1, k1, p1, then begin again until you reach the end of the row." The part of the instruction in parentheses therefore indicates that these stitches alone are to be repeated three times before returning to the instructions immediately following the asterisk.

KNITTING THE PIECES

TIPS
1. Where instructions call for several rows to be repeated a specific number of times, for example between increase rows when shaping a sleeve, tick off each row as you complete it until each row on the pattern is marked with the correct number of ticks. Then if you need to make a matching piece such as a second sleeve, turn each tick into a cross as you complete the row.
2. When a pattern requires you to change to another needle size (always at the end of a row), lay aside the empty needle and pick up one needle of the new size. Work one row, thus transferring your knitting to the new needle. Then lay aside the other old-size needle and pick up the second new-size needle to continue the work.

The usual working order for a garment is: back, front (or left front, right front), sleeves, followed by any neckband or other borders, which may be described separately or under a general heading such as "finishing" or "assembly."

Always work the pieces in the order given. This usually begins with the back, which tends to involve the least shaping, making it easier for the knitter to become familiar with a stitch pattern before progressing to pieces with more complicated shapes. Some knitters like to make one sleeve next, just to check they have sufficient yarn for the garment—the back plus one sleeve make up approximately one half the yarn required for the garment, allowing, too, for extra yarn for bands, borders, pockets, and so on. If the pieces are not laid out in the order just outlined, there is probably a good reason for this. For example, a sweater with a patterned front and a plain back might begin with instructions for the front and then instruct you to work the back to a matching length, sometimes involving a different number of rows.

Begin at the beginning. Start with the correct needles and yarn and cast on the number of stitches required for your size. Recount the stitches to ensure they are correct, then begin to knit.

Check row and stitch count. Whenever a row or stich count is given, count the rows and stitches you have made to ensure they are correct. You may find a row counter (page 15) useful. Check off each section on the pattern as you complete it, or keep a record in your notebook. Pieces made to match in length, for example a front and a back made to match at the underarm seam, should be worked with exactly the same number of rows in the corresponding sections unless the pattern states otherwise. Where a pattern requires you to work to a certain length, keep a note of the number of rows you worked on the first piece so that you can match the second piece exactly

Measure your work in progress. Instructions often ask you to "continue until work measures x in. (y cm)." To measure the length of work on the needles, lay the piece on a flat surface without stretching it and measure the length at the center (see left). It is impossible to measure the width of a piece of knitting accurately while it is on the needles. That's why correct gauge is so important. If you are sure that your gauge is correct, you do not need to check the width.

Complete each section in turn. Block the piece (pages 40–41) and leave it to dry. Check the measurements before beginning the next piece.

Finish your garment. Assemble the garment according to the instructions.

HOLDING STITCHES

To shape a neck edge or pocket opening, stitches may be left on a holder to be worked into again at a later stage. A stitch holder (page 15) often takes the form of a large metal or plastic safety pin with a blunt point.

STEP 1 Open the holder and slip the required stitches onto the pin, inserting the pin from right to left without twisting the stitches.

STEP 2 Close the holder. The stitches will not unravel. When you return to these stitches to continue working on them, you may be able to open the holder and work directly from it, but you will usually find that the holder closure is not at the side where you want to begin. Slip the stitches from the holder onto a spare needle, then work them as directed.

TIPS
1. To hold a few stitches, you can use an ordinary large safety pin but take care not to split the stitches with the sharp point.
2. To hold a large number of stitches, or stitches around a shaped edge that will not sit easily on a straight pin, use a length of yarn. Thread a blunt-tipped needle with a length of smooth contrasting yarn and slip the needle through the required stitches. Knot the yarn ends together to prevent unraveling. When you return to the stitches, slip them onto a spare needle, beginning at the side opposite to where you want to begin working and remove the spare yarn.

CORRECTING MISTAKES

Lay your work flat from time to time, right side up, and take a good look at it. The sooner you spot a mistake in a pattern or an incorrect stitch, the less time it takes to fix it.

CROCHET HOOK METHOD

Use this method to correct a single wrong stitch in stockinette stitch, for example a knit stitch made on a purl row (showing a purl bump on the right side) or a stitch that splits the yarn.

STEP 1 With the right side of the work facing up, work along the next row to the stitch above the mistake. Drop this stitch from the left needle and unravel it down to the correct stitch just below the mistake. Insert a crochet hook into the loop of this stitch, inserting it from front to back. The crochet hook size should not be larger than the needles you are using.

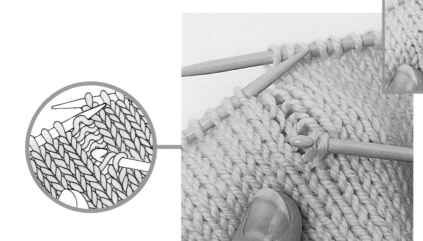

STEP 2 Insert the crochet hook under the strand of thread immediately above the loop on the hook and catch it in the hook. Pull the strand through the loop on the hook.

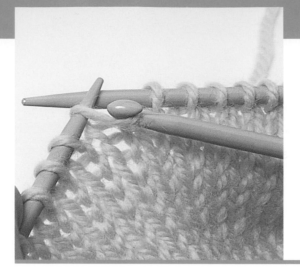

STEP 3
Repeat step 2 until all the strands have been hooked up. Slip the last loop onto the left needle without twisting it. Complete the row.

UNRAVELING METHOD
Use this method where a mistake has been made in shaping or in a complicated stitch pattern.

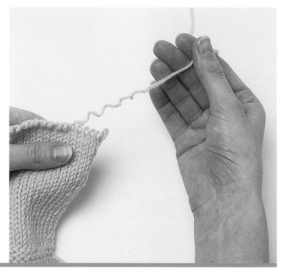

STEP 1
Slip the stitches off the needle and unravel the work down to one row above the mistake. Hold the work in your left hand and a needle in your right hand that is a few sizes smaller than your knitting needles.

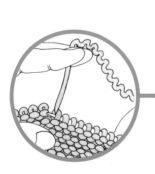

STEP 2
Insert the needle tip, from back to front and from right to left, into the stitch below the first empty loop, then pull gently on the yarn to unravel the loop. Pick up each stitch in turn along the row in this way, unraveling the incorrect row. Using the correct needle size, work the next row. Then discard the (now empty) smaller needle and pick up the other correct needle.

SELVAGE STITCHES

Pattern instructions often include instructions for selvage stitches. A selvage is one or more stitches at the side edge of a piece of knitting worked in a different manner to the main stitch pattern. Selvages make the edges neater, firmer, and less liable to curl. On a free edge, such as a band or border, they may also be decorative. When working stitch patterns, selvage stitches are added to the number of stitches required for the repeating pattern. Pieces with selvage stitches are usually joined with a mattress stitch (pages 42–43), to conceal the selvages in the seam and achieve a professional result.

SIMPLE GARTER STITCH SELVAGE

This is the most common selvage used on stockinette stitch fabrics and other stitch patterns where pieces are to be joined using a mattress stitch (pages 42 43). It makes the edge stitches slightly firmer, avoiding an uneven appearance. To work this selvage, simply work the first and last stitch of every row as a knit stitch.

CHAIN STITCH SELVAGE

This selvage is used to form a neat edge on garter stitch (all rows knit), where both edges will be left free, as for a strap, or only one edge will be left free, as at the front edge of a cardigan.

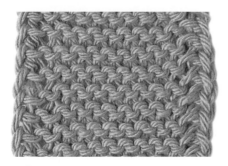

Chain stitch selvage on both edges

Row 1 Bring the yarn forward in front of the right needle, insert the right needle into the first stitch from right to left (purlwise) and slip the first stitch onto the right needle (abbreviated **sl 1 p-wise wyif**). Take the yarn to the back between the needles and knit to the end of the row. Repeat this row.

Chain stitch selvage on one edge

Row 1 Repeat row 1 above.
Row 2 Knit to end.
Repeat these 2 rows. The chain stitch selvage is formed at the beginning of Row 1.

PROJECT 3 — TANK TOP

Now that you have learned not only the basic techniques, but also how to check your gauge, sew a seam, and read a pattern, you can make this easy tank top. Using extra-chunky yarn and giant needles, it will grow very quickly. Choose your favorite color from the large range available.

SIZES

to fit bust/chest	32	34	36	38	in.
	81	86	92	97	cm
actual measurement	36	38	40	42	in.
	91	96	102	107	cm
length to shoulder	19	19	19½	19½	in.
	48	48	50	50	cm

MATERIALS

COLINETTE YARNS POINT FIVE (APPROX. 54 YDS/50 M PER 100 G BALL)

COLOR Sahara 4[4 5 5] 100-g hanks
NEEDLES sizes 17 (12 mm) and 15 (10 mm)
large knitter's sewing-up needle

GAUGE

Required gauge over stockinette is 8 sts and approximately 12 rows to 4 in. (10 cm). Using size 17 (12 mm) needles, cast on about 12 stitches. Work in stockinette stitch for 16 rows. Cast off. Block and press the sample using the warm-steam method (page 41), then measure the gauge (pages 50–51).

If you have more stitches or rows than recommended, your gauge is too tight and you should try another sample using larger needles. If you have fewer stitches or rows than recommended, your gauge is too loose and you should try another sample using smaller needles.

ABBREVIATIONS

k—knit; **p**—purl; **st(s)**—stitch(es); **g.st.**—garter stitch (all rows knit); **in.**—inches; **cm**—centimeters.

TIP

This type of bulky yarn is not suitable for sewing long seams because the loosely twisted parts will tend to break, so use an oddment of finer yarn in a toning color to sew the side seams. If possible, this yarn should be 100 percent wool, like the knitting yarn.

NOTES

1. Instructions in brackets [ ] refer to the 3 larger sizes. Where only one figure is shown this refers to all sizes. You may wish to photocopy the instructions and highlight all the figures that refer to your chosen size.
2. Before commencing, wind the yarn into balls (pages 12–13).

BACK

Using size 15 (10 mm) needles cast on 36[38, 40, 42] sts.

Work in g.st. for 3 rows.

Change to size 17 (12 mm) needles.

Work in stockinette (1 row k, 1 row p) until the work measures 10[10, 10½, 10½] in./26[26, 27, 27] cm from cast-on edge, ending with a p row.

Make a note of the number of stockinette rows you have worked from the last row of g.st.

SHAPE ARMHOLES

Next row Bind off first 4 sts, k to end. 32[34, 36, 38] sts remain.

Following row Bind off first 4 sts purlwise, p to end. 28[30, 32, 34] sts remain.

Continue in stockinette (beginning with a k row) until work measures 18[18, 18½, 18½] in./45[45, 47, 47] cm) from cast-on edge, ending with a k row.

Make a note of the number of stockinette rows you have worked from the last row of g.st.

Change to size 15 (10 mm) needles.

Work in g.st. for 3 rows.

Change to size 17 (12 mm) needles and bind off.

Cut yarn leaving a 10 in. (25 cm) tail.

FRONT

Work exactly as given for Back, matching the noted number of rows for each part.

ASSEMBLY

Use the warm-steam method (page 41) to block and press Front and Back. Avoid g.st. edging.

With right sides of Front and Back together, use yarn ends from casting off to join shoulders for 2½ in. (6.5 cm) on each side with mattress stitch (pages 42–43), inserting needle through centers of bound-off loops to make the seam less bulky.

ARMHOLE BORDERS MAKE 2

See pages 46–47 for pick up and knit methods. This yarn is particularly bulky, so when picking

up sts along side edges of armholes insert needle through center of first st of row (instead of between first and second sts).

With the right side of the work facing you, using size 15 (10 mm) needles, beginning at the underarm, pick up and knit 4 sts from 4 bound-off sts of armhole shaping. Pick up and knit 18[18, 20, 20] sts evenly up first side of armhole edge to shoulder seam. Pick up and knit another 18[18, 20, 20] sts down second side of armhole edge to corner. Pick up and knit 4 sts from 4 bound-off sts. 44[44, 48, 48] sts.

K 1 row.

Change to a size 17 (12 mm) needle and bind off.

Cut yarn leaving a 4 in. (10 cm) tail.

Join side seams using mattress stitch (pages 42–43) and toning yarn, working through the center of the edge sts as given for bulky yarn.

Run in all the ends on wrong side of work (page 45).

SHAPING

Knitted pieces can be shaped in various ways as the work proceeds. The simplest way to increase knitting width is to increase the needle size. This method is often used just after a lower border or cuff, making the main part of the work looser and therefore wider. However, changing needle sizes intermittently throughout a knitted piece can result in a very uneven appearance. Therefore the number of stitches must be adjusted instead. The most common shaping methods are "increasing" (extra stitches make the fabric wider) and "decreasing" (fewer stitches make the fabric narrower).

INCREASING

There are several ways to make an extra stitch, the simplest of which is the "yarn over" increase (**yo**—page 89). This extra stitch creates a hole in the knitting, so other methods are used for a neater finish. The two most common methods for increasing a single stitch are shown below.

BAR INCREASE (KNIT INTO FRONT AND BACK OF ONE STITCH, ABBREVIATED **kfb**)
This is a neat increase, which makes a little horizontal bar beneath the extra stitch, making it easy to count the number of increases made. It is usually used at the side edges of the work where it will be disguised by the seam.

This increase is shown here at the beginning of a row, although it may also be worked at the end.

 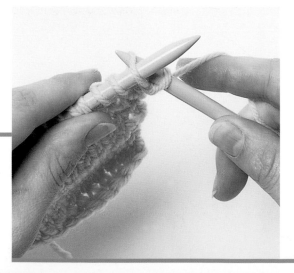

STEP 1 Knit one stitch in the usual way, but without slipping it off the left needle. Insert the tip of the right needle into the back of the same stitch, that is, from right to left as shown.

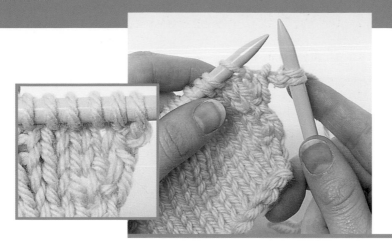

STEP 2 Wrap the yarn round the right needle tip and pull the new stitch through, this time slipping the stitch off the left needle. Two stitches have been created on the right needle. The increase is visible as a little bar beneath the second stitch.

MAKE 1 (MAKE ONE BY LIFTING A THREAD AND KNITTING INTO IT THROUGH THE BACK OF THE LOOP, ABBREVIATED **m1 tbl**) This method is useful when increasing in the middle of a row or when increasing several stitches evenly spaced across a row. It may also be worked one or two stitches in from the side edges for a very neat finish. The extra stitch sits neatly between two stitches of the row below. This increase is shown here worked in the middle of a row.

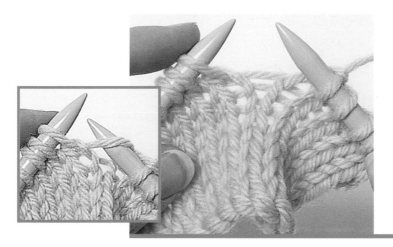

STEP 1 Work to the position where the extra stitch is required. Hold the needles a short distance apart and you will see a horizontal strand of yarn across the gap. Insert the tip of the right needle under this horizontal strand.

STEP 2 Transfer the strand to the left needle, inserting the tip of the left needle from front to back.

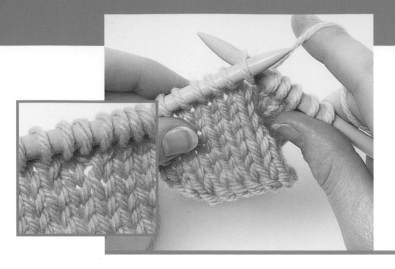

STEP 3 Insert the tip of the right needle into the back of this new stitch, from right to left as shown, and knit it in the usual way. The extra stitch blends into the knitting.

SIMPLE CAST-ON

Sometimes a group of several stitches must be added at a side edge, or a group of bound-off stitches replaced. The simple cast-on is shown here at a side edge.

STEP 1 Hold the needle with the stitches in your right hand and wrap the yarn counterclockwise around the left thumb.

STEP 2 Insert the tip of the right needle from right to left into the loop on the thumb.

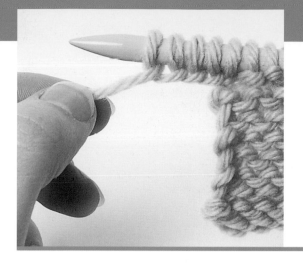

STEP 3 Slip the loop onto the right needle and pull to tighten gently. The new stitch should not be too tight or it will be difficult to work into on the next row.

Repeat steps 1–3 as many times as required.

DECREASING

There are several ways of working two or more stitches together. The four methods outlined below are the most common.

SLIP ONE, KNIT ONE, PASS SLIP STITCH OVER (ABBREVIATED **SKP** OR **sl 1, k1, psso**) The resulting decrease slopes from bottom right to top left. Shown here worked at the beginning of a row.

STEP 1 Insert the tip of the right needle into the first stitch from left to right as if to knit it, then slip it onto the right needle without working it.

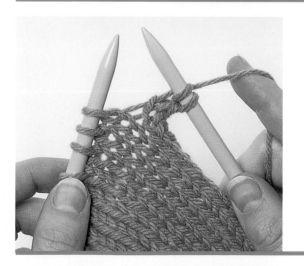

STEP 2 Knit the next stitch.

STEP 3 Insert the tip of the left needle into the slipped stitch from left to right.

STEP 4 Lift the slipped stitch over the knitted stitch and off the right needle, in the same way as when binding off.

STEP 5 One stitch remains on the right needle. One stitch has been decreased.

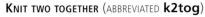

KNIT TWO TOGETHER (ABBREVIATED **k2tog**)

This decrease produces a stitch that slopes from bottom left to top right. It is shown here worked at the end of a row:

STEP 1 Insert the tip of the right needle from left to right (knitwise) through two stitches together on the left needle.

STEP 2 Knit these two stitches together in the same way as when knitting one stitch. One stitch has been decreased.

PAIRED DECREASES

Where instructions ask you to "decrease 1 stitch at each end" of several right side rows, the two methods above may be paired to make matching edges.

If you use the "slip 1, knit 1, pass slipped stitch over" (**SKP**—pages 65–66) at the beginning of each right-side row and K2tog at the end, as shown above, the result will be neatly decreased edges with matching slopes.

DECREASING ON EVERY ROW

Sometimes it is necessary to decrease on every row, including wrong-side rows. The next two decreases are often used in this way. They are also sometimes used when decreasing over a stitch pattern, to blend in with the pattern.

Purl two together (abbreviated **p2tog**)

Worked on a wrong-side row, this decrease produces a stitch that slopes from bottom left to top right on the right side of the work, thus matching "knit 2 together" (**k2tog**— page 67) in appearance. It is shown here at the beginning of a purl row.

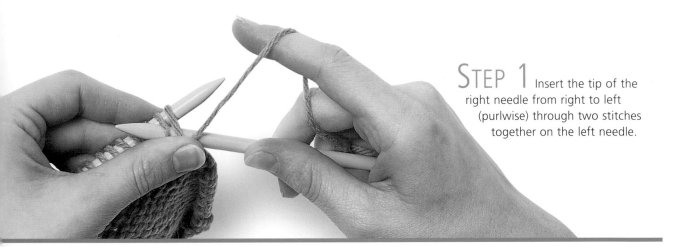

STEP 1 Insert the tip of the right needle from right to left (purlwise) through two stitches together on the left needle.

STEP 2 Wrap the yarn counterclockwise around the tip of the right needle.

STEP 3 And purl the two stitches together in the same way as when purling one stitch. One stitch has been decreased.

Purl two together through back loops
(abbreviated **p2tog tbl**)
Worked on a wrong side row, this decrease produces a stitch that slopes from bottom right to top left on the right side of the work, thus matching "slip 1, knit 1, pass slipped stitch over" (**SKP**—pages 65–66) in appearance. This is shown here worked at the end of a purl row.

STEP 1 Insert the tip of the right needle from the back of the work, left to right through two stitches together on the left needle.

STEP 2 Wrap the yarn counterclockwise around the tip of the right needle, in the same way as for a purl stitch.

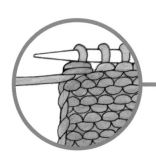

STEP 3 And purl the two stitches together in the same way as when purling one stitch. One stitch has been decreased.

STORING WORK IN PROGRESS

Between knitting sessions, your work should be stored away from dust, damp, and excessive heat or sunlight. Use a bag, box, or drawer that is smooth inside to prevent snagging—woven baskets should be lined with fabric. A small box or pouch is useful for items such as tape measures, scissors, notebooks, pencils, and so on.
Never put your knitting aside halfway through a row. The stitches at the point where you leave off will tend to stretch unevenly.

Place the needles side by side. If you have quite a lot of stitches and they are liable to slip off, use point protectors (page 15), or use a rubber band tightly and wind it so that it binds both needle points together. **Never** push the needles into the ball of yarn or into the work as this will damage strands of yarn or stitches.

KEEPING PATTERNS CONSTANT

When decreasing (or increasing) at the same time as working in a stitch pattern, it is important to keep the stitch pattern correct. A stitch pattern as written row by row at the beginning of knitting instructions will not always fit into the differing numbers of stitches on each row as shaping proceeds. The instructions for the Block Pattern piece shown below might read "keeping pattern constant, decrease 1 stitch at each end next and every other row."

Learn to look at the stitch you are working and understand how it is constructed. In this Block Pattern example, each block consists of three stitches

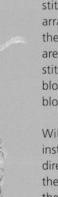

and four rows. These blocks of stockinette stitch and reverse stockinette stitch are arranged in a checkerboard fashion. So as the shaping proceeds, blocks at the edges are reduced from three stitches to two stitches, then to one stitch, then the next block of three stitches becomes the edge block, but the pattern remains constant.

With complicated stitch patterns, the instructions usually include row-by-row directions for the shaping rows. Follow these instructions carefully and examine the result closely to make sure your interpretation is correct.

Fully-fashioned shaping may be used to emphasize seams more strongly, usually on garments worked in lightweight yarns.

This example also includes a garter stitch selvage at each side.

On right-side rows K2, SKP, k to last 4 sts, k2tog, k2.

On wrong-side rows K1, p to last st, k1. The fully fashioned shaping may be made wider by working more stitches between the edges and the decreases.

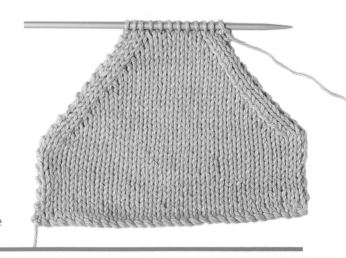

PROJECT 4
FAMILY SWEATER

This casual sweater with an easy rib pattern is styled in five generous sizes to suit most members of the family.

SIZES

to fit chest	28/30	32/34	36	38/40	42/44	in.
	71/76	81/86	92	97/102	107/112	cm
actual	33¾	37	40½	44	47½	in.
measurement	85.5	94	103	112	120.5	cm
length	19	22	24	25	26	in.
to shoulder	48	56	61	63.5	66	cm
sleeve seam	14	16½	17½	18	18½	in.
	35.5	42	44.5	46	47	cm

MATERIALS

SIRDAR DENIM CHUNKY (APPROX. 171 YDS/156 M PER 100 G BALL)
COLOR faded denim (shade 567) 4[5 6 7 8] 100-g balls
NEEDLES sizes 10 (6 mm) and 8 (5 mm)

GAUGE

Required gauge over Broken Rib Pattern is 14 sts and 19 rows to 4 in. (10 cm). Using size 10 (6 mm) needles, cast on 19 sts and work 22 rows Broken Rib Pattern as below. Measure gauge (pages 50–51).

If your gauge is tight, with more sts or rows to 4 in. (10 cm), try another test-piece with larger needles. If your gauge is loose, with fewer sts or rows to 4 in. (10 cm), try again with smaller needles.

ABBREVIATIONS

k—knit; p—purl; rep—repeat; st(s)—stitch(es); inc—increase; k2tog—knit 2 together; SKP—slip one, knit one, pass slip stitch over; p2tog—purl 2 together; m1 tbl make one through back loop; in.—inches; cm—centimeters.

BACK

Using size 8 (5 mm) needles cast on 61[67, 73, 79, 85] sts.
Rib row 1 *P1, k2, rep from * to last st, p1.
Rib row 2 *K1, p2, rep from * to last st, k1.

Rep these 2 rows twice more. 6 rib rows. Change to size 10 (6 mm) needles.
Broken Rib Pattern
Row 1 *P1, k5, rep from * to last st, p1.
Row 2 P to end.
Rep these 2 rows until Back measures 11¼[13¼, 14½, 14½, 15½] in./28.5[33.5, 37, 37, 39.5] cm in all, ending row 2. Make a note of the number of pattern rows you have worked.
Place a marker at each end of the last row. **
Continue in pattern as established until Back measures 19[22, 24, 25, 26] in./48[56, 61, 63.5, 66] cm in all ending row 2. Note that stitch pattern should remain constant throughout. Make a note of the number of rows above the markers.

Shape Shoulders

Keeping pattern constant, bind off 11[12, 13, 14, 15] sts at beginning next 2 rows (knitwise on right-side row, purlwise on wrong side row).
Bind off 11[12, 13, 14, 16] sts at beginning following 2 rows, in the same way.
Bind off remaining 17[19, 21, 23, 23] sts knitwise.

FRONT

Work as given for Back to **.
Continue in pattern as established for 12[14, 16, 16, 16] rows less than rows worked on Back above markers, ending row 2.
Shape Front Neck: First Side
1st row Pattern as established for 27[29, 31, 33, 36] sts, turn. Work on these sts only:
2nd row P1, p2tog, p to end.
3rd row Pattern as established to last 3 sts, k2tog, k1.
4th and 5th rows Rep 2nd and 3rd rows.
6th row Rep 2nd row. 22[24, 26, 28, 31] sts remain.
Continue in pattern as established on these sts for a further 6[8, 10, 10, 10] rows, ending p row.
Shape Shoulder
Next row Bind off 11[12, 13, 14, 15] sts knitwise, pattern as established to end.
Following row P to end.
Bind off remaining 11[12, 13, 14, 16] sts leaving a

10 in. (25 cm) tail.

Second Side

With right side of Front facing, rejoin yarn at right of remaining sts.

1st row Bind off 7[9, 11, 13, 13] sts at center front and complete the row in pattern as established. 27[29, 31, 33, 36] sts.

2nd row P to last 3 sts, p2tog tbl, p1.

3rd row K1, SKP, pattern as established to end.

4th and 5th rows Rep 2nd and 3rd rows.

6th row Rep 2nd row. 22[24, 26, 28, 31] sts remain.

Continue in pattern as established on these sts for a further 7[9, 11, 11, 11] rows, ending right-side row.

Shape Shoulder

Next row Bind off 11[12, 13, 14, 15] sts purlwise, p to end.

Following row Pattern as established.

Bind off remaining 11[12, 13, 14, 16] sts leaving a 10 in. (25 cm) tail.

SLEEVES MAKE 2

Using size 8 (5 mm) needles cast on 25[31, 31, 37, 37] sts.

Rep rib rows 1 and 2 as for Back, 4 times in all. 8 rib rows.

Change to size 10 (6 mm) needles.

1st row P1, (m1 tbl, k1) twice, m1 tbl, *p1, k5, rep from * to last 4 sts, p1, (m1 tbl, k1) twice, m1 tbl, p1. 31[37, 37, 43, 43] sts.

2nd row P to end.

3rd row *P1, k5, rep from * to last st, p1.

4th row P to end.

Shape Sleeve

Keep pattern constant while increasing as follows:

Next row P1, m1 tbl, pattern as established to last st, m1 tbl, p1.

Work 3 rows in pattern as established. 33[39, 39, 45, 45] sts.

Rep these 4 rows 11[11, 14, 14, 14] more times. 55[61, 67, 73, 73] sts.

Continue in pattern as established until Sleeve measures 14[16½, 17½, 18, 18½] in./ 35.5[42, 44.5, 46, 47] cm, or length required, ending p row.

Bind off knitwise.

COLLAR

Using size 8 (5 mm) needles cast on 65[71, 77, 80, 83] sts.

Rep rib rows 1 and 2 as for Back until Collar measures 4[4½, 5, 5, 5] in./10[11, 12.5, 12.5, 12.5] cm ending rib row 2.

Change to a size 10 (6 mm) needle and bind off, working each st in k or p as established.

ASSEMBLY

Block all pieces except Collar using water-spray method (page 41).

Join shoulder seams with backstitch (pages 44–45) using tails left for this purpose, matching pattern. Fold one Sleeve in half to find center of top edge. Matching this point to shoulder seam, join top edge of Sleeve between markers on side edges (page 44). Sew on other Sleeve in same way. Join side and sleeve seams using mattress stitch (pages 42–43).

Fold Collar in half to find center of cast-on edge. Matching this point to center back, join cast-on edge of Collar to neck opening, with sides meeting at center front, so that when Collar is folded over, mainly knit side is uppermost. At center front, join side edges of Collar for ¾ in. (2 cm).

KNITTING IN THE ROUND

Knitting may be worked in the form of a seamless tube, ideal for neckbands, when the stitches are picked up around the neck edge as on page 46. The technique may also be used to construct other shapes, such as sleeves, gloves, hats, and socks, and it is often a strong element in the traditional knitting of various countries. Knitting in the round (circular knitting) is worked on a circular needle or on a set of double-pointed needles.

Circular needles consist of a rigid pointed section at each end joined by a flexible length of plastic or wire. They are available in all the usual sizes and several lengths. Choose the correct size to suit your yarn and pattern, in a length somewhat shorter than the circumference of the work. The length of a circular needle is measured from needle tip to needle tip. Too long a needle will stretch the work and be difficult to use. A suitable length for most adult neckbands is 16 in. (40 cm). Long length circular needles are sometimes used to knit extra-large items "to and fro" in the usual way, because the weight of the knitting may then be supported in the lap instead of weighing down the ends of a long pair of needles.

Sets of double-pointed needles are particularly useful for working with small numbers of stitches, for example a child's neckband or the shaping at the top of a hat. Sets of four or five are available in all the usual sizes and various lengths. Choose a length to suit the number of stitches; if the needles are too short the stitches will tend to slip off the ends.

WORKING ON A CIRCULAR NEEDLE

Circular needles are ideal for knitting larger items in the round. To start, you cast on in the usual way, then bring the needle ends together and knit.

STEP 1 Cast on in the same way as for straight knitting (pages 20–23). Spread the stitches evenly around the needle; they should not be stretched. Turn the work around so the needle tip with the last cast-on stitch is in your right hand and the tip with the first stitch in your left. Slip a plastic ring marker, or a loop of contrast yarn, onto the tip of the right needle to mark the end of every round. Before knitting the first round, make sure that the stitches are not twisted round on the needle (see opposite).

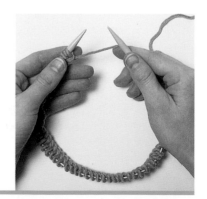

TIPS

1. When you are working circular knitting, the right side of the work is always facing you.
2. If a plastic circular needle is stiff and curly after storage, soak it in warm water for a few minutes then straighten it between your fingers.

STEP 2

Work into the first cast-on stitch rather tightly to close the gap. Continue working around the stitches in the required stitch pattern, regularly pushing new stitches away from the right needle tip and pushing the stitches to be worked toward the left needle tip.

STEP 3

When you reach the marker, one round is complete. Slip the marker from the left needle tip to the right tip to begin the next round. Working all the stitches as knit stitches on every round produces stockinette stitch with the knit side facing you.

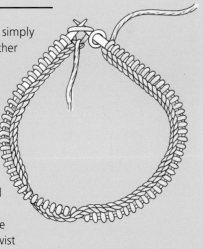

AVOIDING TWISTED STITCHES

When knitting with circular needles, you simply cast on then bring the needle ends together and knit. But before knitting the first round, you must make sure that the stitches are not twisted on the needle. If the stitches are twisted as shown right, hold the needle tips apart and arrange the stitches so that the cast-on edge is inside the circle, all the way around. Check again when you've worked the first round, or you could end up with a permanently twisted loop of knitting instead of a tube. Once you have started to knit, you cannot correct the twist without unraveling the knitting.

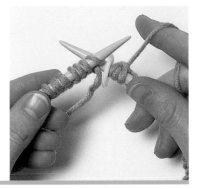

WORKING ON DOUBLE-POINTED NEEDLES

Double-pointed needles are used most often for small items, such as mittens or socks. But you can use as many double-pointed needles as you need for a larger project.

STEP 1 Cast on the required number of stitches onto three needles from a set of four (or four needles from a set of five). The extra needle will be used to begin the first round. Divide the number of stitches evenly between the needles. Arrange the needles as shown (or in a square for four needles) with the cast-on edge untwisted, the first cast-on stitch at the tip of the left needle, and the yarn ball at the right needle tip. Place a plastic ring marker or a loop of contrast yarn on the tip of the right needle.

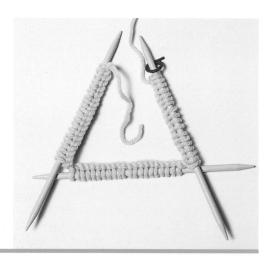

STEP 2 Use the empty (fourth or fifth) needle to work rather tightly into the first stitch on the left needle to close the gap. Work all the stitches on this needle in the stitch pattern required. Then use this empty needle to work all the stitches on the next needle, and so on. When you reach the marker, one round is complete. Slip the marker from the left needle to the right needle to begin the next round.

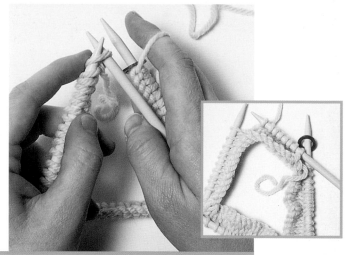

TIP
If the marker tends to slip off the needle, place it between the last two stitches on the needle. The last stitch of the round will then be the stitch after the marker.

SWEATER AND HAT

Knit this fun sweater with differently striped sleeves (or make both sleeves alike if you wish). The roll neck is worked in the round for a neat finish. The matching hat is also worked in the round to avoid a seam.

SIZES

SWEATER

to fit bust/chest	30	32	34	36	in.
	76	81	86	92	cm
actual measurement	34	36	38	40	in.
	86	92	97	102	cm
length to shoulder	22	23	24	25	in.
	56	58.5	61	63.5	cm
sleeve seam	14½	16	17½	19	in.
	36.5	40.5	44	48	cm

HAT

to fit head	21		23		in.
	53.5		58.5		cm

MATERIALS

FOR THE SWEATER

ROWAN POLAR (APPROX. 109 YDS/100 M PER 100 G BALL)

COLOR A lettuce (shade 642) 5[5 6 6] 100-g balls

COLOR B aerial (shade 648) 1[1 1 1]

COLOR C winter white (shade 645) 1[1 1 1]

small amount of finer yarn to match col.A, for sewing up

NEEDLES sizes 11 (8 mm) and 10½ (6½ mm)

set of 4 (or 5) double-pointed needles size 11 (7 mm)

2 stitch holders

FOR THE HAT (SMALL AMOUNTS OF YARN REMAINING FROM THE SWEATER MAY BE SUFFICIENT)

COLOR A lettuce (shade 642) ½[1] 100-g ball

approx. ⅓ ball each of col.B aerial (shade 648) and col.C winter white (shade 645)

NEEDLES set of 4 (or 5) double-pointed needles size 10½ (6½ mm)

GAUGE

Required gauge over stockinette is 12 sts and 16 rows to 4 in. (10 cm). Using size 11 (8 mm) needles, cast on 18 sts and work 24 rows stockinette. Measure gauge (pages 50–51).

If your gauge is tight, with more sts or rows to 4 in. (10 cm), try another test-piece with larger needles. If your gauge is loose, with fewer sts or rows to 4 in. (10 cm), try again with smaller needles.

ABBREVIATIONS

k—knit; **p**—purl; **rep**—repeat; **st(s)**—stitch(es); **inc**—increase; **dec**—decrease; **m1 tbl**—make one through back loop; **SKP**—slip one, knit one, pass slip st over; **k2tog**—knit 2 together; **col.**—color; **in.**—inches; **cm**—centimeters.

NOTES

1. No selvage stitches are given in these instructions, because this is a bulky yarn. When seaming, take one whole stitch from each edge as a seam allowance for a neat finish. For a less bulky finish, take one half stitch from each edge as a seam allowance.
2. Instructions in brackets [ ] refer to the 3 larger sizes of Sweater, 1 larger size of Hat. Where only one set of figures is given, this refers to all sizes.
3. Sweater in photograph is 2nd size; for other sizes, the Wide Stripe Sleeve color sequence is different.

SWEATER BACK

Using size 10½ (6½ mm) needles and col.A cast on 50[52, 56, 58] sts.

Rib row 1 *K1, p1, rep from * to end.

Rep this row 5 more times. 6 rib rows in all.

Change to size 11 (8 mm) needles.

1st and 3rd Sizes only

Next row K1, m1 tbl, k to end.

2nd and 4th Sizes only

Next row K1, m1 tbl, k to last st, m1 tbl, k1.

All Sizes

51[54, 57, 60] sts.

Work in stockinette, beg with a p row, until Back measures 14[15,15½, 16½] in./35.5[38, 39.5, 42] cm in all, ending with a P row. (Make a note of the number of stockinette rows.)

Shape Armholes

dec row 1 SKP, k to last 2 sts, k2tog.

dec row 2 P to end.

Rep these 2 rows twice more. 45[48, 51, 54] sts. *

Continue in stockinette until Back measures 22[23, 24, 25] in./ 56[58.5, 61, 63.5] cm in all ending with a p row. (Make a note of the number of rows worked after the last dec row).

Shape Shoulders

Bind off 7[8, 8, 9] sts at beginning next 2 rows, knitwise on k row and purlwise on p row.

Bind off 7[7, 8, 8] sts at beginning following 2 rows. 17[18, 19, 20] sts remain.

Slip these sts onto a stitch holder and cut yarn leaving a 10 in. (25 cm) tail.

SWEATER FRONT

Work as given for Back to * matching number of rows exactly.

Continue in stockinette for 10 rows less than Back at beginning of shoulder shaping, ending with a p row.

Shape Front Neck: First Side

1st row K 18[19, 20, 21] sts, turn. Work on these sts only:

2nd row P to end.

3rd row K to last 2 sts, k2tog.

Rep 2nd and 3rd rows 3 more times. 14[15, 16, 17] sts remain.

10th row P to end. Number of rows now matches Back at beginning of shoulder shaping.

Shape Shoulder

Bind off 7[8, 8, 9] sts at beginning next row, k to end.

P 1 row, then bind off remaining 7[7, 8, 8] sts. Cut yarn leaving a 10 in. (25 cm) tail.

Second Side

With right side of work facing, slip 9[10, 11, 12] sts at center front onto a stitch holder. Rejoin col.A at right of remaining 18[19, 20, 21] sts.

1st row K to end.

2nd row P to end.

3rd row SKP, k to end.

4th row P to end.

Rep 3rd and 4th rows 3 more times. 14[15, 16, 17] sts.

11th row K to end.

Shape Shoulder

Bind off 7[8, 8, 9] sts purlwise at beginning next row, p to end.

K 1 row, then bind off remaining 7[7, 8, 8] sts. Cut yarn leaving a 10 in. (25 cm) tail.

NARROW STRIPE SLEEVE

Using size 10½ (6½ mm) needles and col.A cast on 32[32, 34, 34] sts.

Rep rib row 1 as for Back, 4 times in all.

Shape Sleeve

Change to size 11 (8 mm) needles. Cut col.A and

join in col.C leaving 4 in. (10 cm) tails.

Row 1 Using C, k1, m1 tbl, k to last st, m1 tbl, k1. 34[34, 36, 36] sts.

Row 2 Leave col.C and join col.A. P to end.

Row 3 Leave col.A and join col.B. K to end.

Row 4 Using C, p to end.

Row 5 Using A, k to end.

Row 6 Using B, p to end.

Stripe Sequence from now on is 1 row C, 1 row A, 1 row B. There is no need to cut and rejoin the colors. At the beginning of each row, carry the new color up the edge of the work from where you left it 2 rows below.

Working in Stripe Sequence as established, complete Sleeve as follows:

** Rep the last 6 rows, 8[8, 9, 9] more times. 50[50, 54, 54] sts. 54[54, 60, 60] stockinette rows in all.

Work 0[6, 6, 6] more rows without shaping. 54[60, 66, 66] stockinette rows in all, ending with a p row.

Shape Top of Sleeve

dec row 1 SKP, k to last 2 sts, k2tog.

dec row 2 P to end.

Rep these 2 rows twice more. 44[44, 48, 48] sts. Bind off loosely using same col as last row. **.

WIDE STRIPE SLEEVE

Using size 10½ (6½ mm) needles and col.A cast on 32[32, 34, 34] sts.

Rep rib row 1 as for Back, 4 times in all.

Shape Sleeve

Change to size 11 (8 mm) needles. At each col. change, cut old col. and join in new col. leaving 4 in. (10 cm) tails (page 31). Cut col.A and join in col.B[B, C, C].

Row 1 Using B[B, C, C], k1, m1 tbl, k to last st, m1 tbl, k1. 34[34, 36, 36] sts.

Work 5 rows stockinette, beginning and ending p row.

Stripe Sequence from now on is:

1st and 2nd sizes only 6 rows C, 6 rows A, 6 rows B.

3rd and 4th sizes only 6 rows A, 6 rows B, 6 rows C.

Working in Stripe Sequence as established, complete as Narrow Stripe Sleeve from ** to **, ending 6 rows col. B[C, B, B].

ASSEMBLY

Run in all yarn ends from stripes along wrong side of rows (page 45). Block pieces using warm-steam method (page 41); do not press heavily on this soft yarn and be sure to avoid ribbing.

Join shoulder seams with backstitch using ends left for this purpose.

For longer seams, use a small amount of finer yarn in a color to match col.A.

Fold one sleeve in half lengthwise to find center of top edge. Matching this point to shoulder seam, join top edge of sleeve to armhole, matching shaping rows (page 44). Join top edge of other sleeve to armhole in same way.

Using mattress stitch (pages 42–43), join sleeve seams, matching stripes. Join side seams.

ROLL NECK

With right side of work facing, using set of 4 (or 5) double-pointed needles size 10½ (6½ mm) and col.A, begin at right shoulder seam: k 17[18, 19, 20] sts from holder at back neck; pick up and k 11 sts from first side of front neck shaping; k 9[10, 11, 12] sts from holder at center front; pick up and k 11 sts from second side of front neck shaping. 48[50, 52, 54] sts. Divide sts evenly between 3 (or 4) needles leaving 4th (5th) needle free to begin work (see pages 74–76 for knitting in the round, pages 46–47 for picking up stitches):

Round 1 K to end.

Rep this round 11 more times. 12 rounds in all, ending level with right shoulder seam.

Change to a size 11 (8 mm) needle and bind off. Cut yarn leaving a 4 in. (10 cm) tail. Run in tail along bound-off edge. Allow neck edge to form a roll.

TIP

To block the hat, press gently using the warm-steam method (page 41), then leave to dry shaped over a kitchen mixing bowl of suitable size. Allow the lower edge to form a roll.

HAT

Using set of 4 (or 5) double-pointed needles size 10½ (6½ mm) and col.A, cast on 68[76] sts. Divide sts evenly between 3 (or 4) needles leaving 4th (5th) needle free to begin work. Place a marker before the last cast-on stitch, to mark last stitch of each round, and slip this marker on every round. When changing cols leave 4 in. (10 cm) tails.

K 12[14] rounds.

Change to col.C.

inc round *K17[19], m1 tbl, rep from * to end. 72[80] sts.

K 5 rounds.

Change to col.B. K 6 rounds.

Change to col.A. K 6 rounds.

Change to col.C. K 1 round.

dec round 1 K 7[8] *SKP, k2tog, k 14[16], rep from * twice more, SKP, k2tog, k 7[8]. 64[72] sts.

K 3 rounds.

dec round 2 K to 1 st before first dec below, *SKP, k2tog, k to 1 st before next dec below, rep from * twice more, SKP, k2tog, k to end of round. 56[64] sts.

Change to col.B. K 1 round.

Next round Rep dec round 2. 48[56] sts.

Rep last 2 rounds twice more. 32[40] sts.

Change to col.A. Rep last 2 rounds, 2[3] more times. 16 sts remain.

Next round *SKP, k2tog, rep from * to end. 8 sts remain. Cut yarn leaving a 6 in. (15 cm) tail and thread through these 8 sts. Pull up tightly and secure end.

Run in all remaining yarn ends on wrong side of rows (page 45).

DETAILS

Borders, neckbands, buttonholes, pockets, and edgings can all be worked in many ways, but the simplest methods are often the neatest. This chapter describes basic techniques that you are likely to encounter in knitting instructions for garments and other items.

NECKBANDS AND BORDERS

Collars, neckbands, cuffs, lower borders, pocket trims, front bands and buttonhole bands, in fact any free edge of knitting that is not to be joined into a seam, are all normally worked in a firm stitch pattern that will not curl. That is why so many garments begin at the lower edge with several rows of rib.

Crew neckband

Collar

Stitches for a **crew neckband** may be picked up (pages 46–47) around the neck edge onto two needles, beginning at one shoulder seam. The rows required are then worked in a rib, or other stitch, and the stitches bound off and the neckband joined with a seam. The stitches may also be picked up with a circular needle, or a set of double-pointed needles, and worked in the round without a seam (pages 74–76). On lightweight garments, such a neckband may be worked to twice the depth required, then folded to the inside and the bound-off edge sewn to the neck edge.

A **collar** may be knitted as a separate piece and sewn to a neck edge or picked up around the neck edge with a circular needle (or set of double-pointed needles) and worked in rows, turning for each new row at the center front.

The **front band of a cardigan** may be worked sideways. Begin by picking up stitches along the front edge, then work a few rows in rib and bind off in rib as set. Armhole edges for sleeveless garments are often worked in the same way.

A **band** may also be worked **lengthwise** and sewn onto a front or other edge. Always slightly stretch the band as you sew it on, to avoid a buckled edge, and stitch it in place before binding off the stitches so that the length may be adjusted exactly to fit.

Front band

Lengthwise band

CHOOSING BUTTONS

Buttons for knitwear should be smooth and rounded. Fancy shapes and corners tend to catch on strands of yarn and spoil your work. For maximum comfort in baby garments choose small flat buttons. Toggles and buttons with shanks, instead of holes, are useful for bulky knits.

TIPS

1. Buy an extra button—sew it onto a card and keep it with your records or sew it inside the side seam of the garment. One day you'll be glad you did!
2. Buy buttons before working the buttonholes. Work a test buttonhole on your gauge sample and take it along when you buy the buttons for the garment, to choose the correct size.

Buttons made of natural materials, such as wood, horn, or mother-of-pearl, often suit natural fiber yarns very well, whereas metallic and jeweled buttons suit more exotic yarns. Glassy and transparent buttons are a useful option if a good color match is unobtainable. Sew on buttons using the same yarn as used for the button band if possible or use matching sewing thread.

BUTTONHOLES

EYELET BUTTONHOLE

This small buttonhole is simply a yarn over (**yo**—page 89) accompanied by a corresponding decrease (pages 65–66). It is shown here worked on a garter stitch band worked lengthwise. It is also suitable for bands worked sideways.

On the buttonhole row, work to the position required for the buttonhole, yo, k2tog (page 67), work to the end of the row. Depending on the stitch pattern in use, the yarn over may be worked in any of the ways shown on pages 89–90, and sometimes p2tog (pages 68–69) is more appropriate than k2tog.

TWO-ROW BUTTONHOLE

This buttonhole is made by binding off two or more stitches, then casting on again to replace them. It may be made to any suitable width. It is also suitable for bands worked sideways.

STEP 1 Work along the row
to the position required for the buttonhole. Working in the stitch pattern as set, bind off the number of stitches required (three stitches shown here) and continue in the pattern to the end of the row.

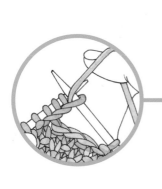

STEP 2 On the following row,
work in the pattern to the bound-off stitches. Turn the work and, using the two-needle method of casting on (pages 20–23), cast on the same number of stitches as you bound off on the previous row. But before slipping the last of these stitches onto the left needle, bring the yarn forward between the needle tips. This tightens the last cast-on stitch and prevents a loose loop from forming.

STEP 3 Turn the
work again so that the cast-on stitches are on the right needle and complete the row. The finished buttonhole is shown here (see far right) on a band of seed stitch (page 37).

SLIT POCKET

There are several different ways of constructing pockets, but this slit pocket is one of the simplest and neatest to use on knitwear, being less bulky than other types.

STEP 1 Knit the pocket lining before working the garment piece it is to be attached to. Normally the pocket lining is worked in stockinette stitch in order to lay as flat as possible when finished. Do not bind off but slip the stitches onto a spare needle.

STEP 2 At the position required for the pocket, on a right-side row, slip a number of stitches matching the pocket lining onto a holder (or bind them off if no pocket trim is required). Then, with the right side of the lining facing, work across the lining stitches from the spare needle and complete the row.

After completing the piece, a pocket trim may be added by working across the stitches left on a holder. Sew down the side edges of the trim along a straight line of stitches.

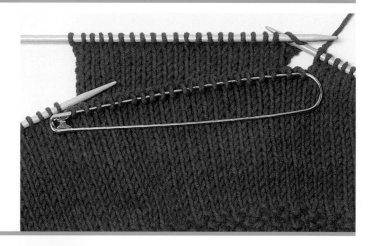

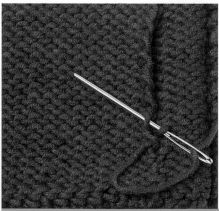

STEP 3 On the wrong side, slip-stitch each side edge of the lining along a straight line of stitches and the lower edge to a straight row of stitches.

SETTING IN ZIPPERS

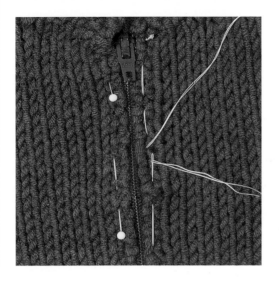

An open-ended zipper may be used to fasten the front edges of a jacket or cardigan, or an ordinary zipper may be stitched into a vertical or horizontal opening worked in the knitting.

With the garment piece(s) right side up on a flat surface, pin the closed zipper underneath the knitting. The edge stitches should be just clear of the zipper teeth, not overlapping them. Do not stretch the knitting. Tack the zipper in place with contrasting sewing thread.

Use matching yarn or sewing thread to backstitch the zipper in place, taking a small backstitch over each row of the edge of the knitting.

TIPS

1. Choose the zipper color to match the garment. If an exact match is unobtainable, choose a darker shade; it will be less noticeable than a zipper in a lighter shade.
2. Knitting should never be stretched to fit a zipper or the result will be a buckled edge. In fact, the knitting should be ¼–½ in. (0.5–1.25 cm) longer than the zipper. Buy the zipper before you complete the knitting, and if necessary adjust the length of the opening to suit.
3. Vertical edges of knitting may be worked with one or more selvage stitches to make a neat finish next to the zipper; a horizontal slit should be bound off and cast on firmly.

PROJECT 6

TODDLER TOP

Great for active kids, with a zip neck, neat collar, and
two pockets: sure to be a favorite!

SIZES

to fit chest	22	24	26	28	in.
	56	61	66	71	cm
actual measurement	26	28	30	32	in.
	66	71	76	81	cm
length to shoulder	13½	16	18	20	in.
	34.5	40.5	45.5	51	cm
sleeve seam with	9¾	11½	13	14½	in.
cuff folded back	24.5	29	33	37	cm

MATERIALS

ROWAN ALL SEASONS COTTON (APPROX. 98 YDS/90 M PER
50 G BALL)
COLOR jaunty (shade 183) 5[6 7 9] 50-g balls
NEEDLES sizes 8 (5 mm) and 7 (4½ mm)
3 stitch holders or spare needles and 2 large
safety pins
zipper length 4 in. (10 cm) to match yarn

GAUGE

Required gauge over stockinette is 16½ sts and 24
rows to 4 in. (10 cm). Using size 8 (5 mm) needles,
cast on 20 sts and work 28 rows stockinette. Measure
gauge (pages 50–51).

NOTES

1. Instructions in brackets [ ] refer to the
3 larger sizes. Where only one set of
figures is given this refers to all sizes.
2. Top in photograph is 2nd size.

If your gauge is tight, with more sts or rows to 4 in.
(10 cm), try another test-piece with larger needles. If
your gauge is loose, with fewer sts or rows to 4 in.
(10 cm), try again with smaller needles.

ABBREVIATIONS

k—knit; **p**—purl; **rep**—repeat; **st(s)**—stitch(es); **inc**—
increase; **k2tog**—knit 2 together; **SKP**—slip one, knit
one, pass slip stitch over; **m1 tbl**—make one through
back loop; **p2tog**—purl 2 together; **p2tog tbl**—purl
2 together through back loops; **sl 1**—slip one;
col.—color; **in.**—inches; **cm**—centimeters.

BACK

Using size 7 (4½ mm) needles cast on 55[59, 63,
67] sts.
Seed St row *K1, p1, rep from * to last st, k1.
Rep this row 3 more times. 4 rows.
Change to size 8 (5 mm) needles.
inc row K1, m1 tbl, k to end. 56[60, 64,
68] sts. **
Work in stockinette beginning p row until Back
measures 7½[10, 11¾, 13½] in./19[25.5, 30,
34.5] cm ending P row. Make a note of the
number of stockinette rows you have worked.
Shape Armholes
Bind off 5 sts at beginning next 2 rows (knitwise
on k row, purlwise on p row). 46[50, 54,
58] sts.
Continue in stockinette until Back measures 13½
[16, 18, 20] in./34.5[40.5, 45.5, 51]cm in all
ending P row. Make a note of the number of
stockinette rows you have worked from
beginning of armhole shaping.

Shape Shoulders

Bind off 7[7, 8, 8] sts at beginning next 2 rows (knitwise on k row, purlwise on p row) and 7[8, 8, 9] sts at beginning following 2 rows.

Slip remaining 18[20, 22, 24] sts onto a stitch holder. Cut yarn leaving a 4 in. (10 cm) tail.

POCKET LININGS MAKE 2

Using size 8 (5 mm) needles cast on 19[21, 23, 25] sts.

Work in stockinette beginning k row for 20[20, 24, 24] rows, ending p row. Cut yarn leaving a 20 in. (50 cm) tail and slip sts onto a stitch holder or spare needle (page 56).

FRONT

Work as given for Back to **.

Work in stockinette beginning p row for 19[19, 23, 23] rows, ending p row.

Place Pockets

Next row K 5 sts, *slip next 19[21, 23, 25] sts onto a stitch holder, then with right side of one pocket lining facing k across 19[21, 23, 25] sts from holder * ; k next 8 sts of Front, then rep * to *; k 5 sts to end.

Continue in stockinette beginning with a p row until length matches Back at beginning of armhole shaping, ending with a p row.

Shape Armholes

Bind off 5 sts at beginning next 2 rows (knitwise on k row, purlwise on p row). 46[50, 54, 58] sts.

Divide for Zipper Opening: First Side

1st row K 23[25, 27, 29] sts, turn. Work on these sts only:

2nd row K1, p to end.

Rep these 2 rows, 11 more times. 24 rows of Opening, ending p row.

Shape Neck

Neck row 1 K 18[20, 21, 23] sts, slip last 5[5, 6, 6] sts onto a stitch holder or large safety pin. Work on remaining sts only:

Neck row 2 P2tog, p to end.

Neck row 3 K to last 2 sts, k2tog.

Rep neck rows 2 and 3, 1[1, 1, 2] more times.

2nd and 3rd Sizes Only

Work neck row 2 once more. K 1 row.

All Sizes

14[15, 16, 17] sts remain. Continue in stockinette, beginning with a p row, until length matches Back at beginning of shoulder shaping, ending with a p row.

Shape Shoulder

Bind off 7[7, 8, 8] sts knitwise at beginning next row.

P 1 row. Bind off remaining 7[8, 8, 9] sts. Cut yarn leaving a 10 in. (25cm) tail.

Zipper Opening: Second Side

With right side of Front facing, rejoin yarn at right of remaining 23[25, 27, 29] sts.

1st row K.

2nd row P to last st, k1.

Rep these 2 rows, 11 more times, and 1st row once again. 25 rows of Opening, ending k row.

Shape Neck

Neck row 1 P 18[20, 21, 23] sts, slip last 5[5, 6, 6] sts onto a stitch holder or large safety pin. Work on remaining sts only:

Neck row 2 K2tog tbl, k to end.

Neck row 3 P to last 2 sts, p2tog tbl.

Rep neck rows 2 and 3, 1[1, 1, 2] more times.

2nd and 3rd Sizes Only

Work neck row 2 once more. P 1 row.

All Sizes

14[15, 16, 17] sts remain. Continue in stockinette, beginning with a k row, until length matches Back at beginning of shoulder shaping, ending with a k row.

Shape Shoulder

Bind off 7[7, 8, 8] sts purlwise at beginning next row.

K 1 row. Bind off remaining 7[8, 8, 9] sts purlwise. Cut yarn leaving a 10 in. (25 cm) tail.

POCKET TRIM MAKE 2

With right side of Front facing, using size 7 (4½ mm) needles, rejoin yarn at right of sts left on holder, work seed st row as for Back across these 19[21, 23, 25] sts.

Rep this row 3 more times. Bind off working k sts purlwise and p sts knitwise to keep pattern constant. Cut yarn leaving a 8 in. (20 cm) tail.

SLEEVES MAKE 2

Using size 7 (4½ mm) needles cast on 29[31, 31, 33] sts.

Rep seed st row as for Back until Sleeve measures 3½ [3½, 4, 4] in./9[9, 10, 10] cm ending wrong-side row.

Change to size 8 (5 mm) needles.

Shape Sleeve

Row 1 K1, m1 tbl, k to last st, m1 tbl, k1.

Work 3[5, 5, 5] rows stockinette, beginning and ending P row. 31[33, 33, 35] sts.

Rep these 4[6, 6, 6] rows 8[8, 9, 9]more times. 47[49, 51, 53] sts.

Continue in stockinette until Sleeve measures 9¾ [11½, 13, 14½] in./ 24.5[29, 33, 37] cm in all with cuff folded in half, ending p row.

Place a marker at each end of last row.

Work a further 6 rows of stockinette, ending p row. Bind off loosely leaving a long tail.

COLLAR

Block Front and Back using wet-spray method (page 41). Join shoulder seams using backstitch (pages 44–45).

With right side of work facing, using size 7 (4½ mm) needles, begin at center front, k across 5[5, 6, 6] sts from holder at second side, pick up and k 11[13, 13, 14] sts from second side of front neck shaping, k across 18[20, 22, 24] sts from holder at center back, pick up and k 10[12, 12, 13] sts from first side of front neck shaping and k across 5[5, 6, 6] sts from holder at first side. 49[55, 59, 63] sts.

Shape Collar Stand

Row 1 K1, p32[36, 39, 43] sts, turn.
Row 2 sl 1 purlwise, k17[19, 21, 23], turn.
Row 3 sl 1 purlwise, p22[24, 26, 28], turn.
Row 4 sl 1 purlwise, k27[29, 31, 33], turn.
Row 5 sl 1 purlwise, p to last st, k1.

Work Seed St row across all sts, as for Back, 16[16, 18, 18] times in all. Change to a size 8 (5 mm) needle and bind off working k sts purlwise and p sts knitwise.

ASSEMBLY

Block Sleeves using wet-spray method (page 41).

Fold one Sleeve in half to find center of top edge. Matching this point to shoulder seam, join top edge of Sleeve to armhole, with rows above markers matching bound-off sts of armhole shapings (page 44). Sew on other Sleeve in same way. Join side and sleeve seams using mattress stitch (pages 42–43).

Sew down pocket linings and side edges of pocket trims (page 84).

Set zipper into front opening (page 85).

Run in any remaining ends.

STITCH LIBRARY

LACE PATTERNS

When working lace patterns, you form the holes (or eyelets) in the knitting by making extra stitches. Each extra stitch is balanced somewhere within the pattern repeat by a corresponding decrease, usually on the same row, so that the number of stitches remains constant over the course of the work. The arrangement of these increases (holes) and decreases, and the methods used for them, determine the appearance of the stitch pattern. In lace knitting, the eyelet holes can be made with either yarn overs or "lifted" stitches.

MAKE ONE STITCH BY YARN OVER (ABBREVIATED **yo**)
A yarn over increase is made simply by winding the yarn once around the right needle. This creates a hole or eyelet in the knitting. Be careful to wind yarn overs correctly, as shown below—if they twist the wrong way, the following row will be difficult to work and the appearance of the stitch pattern will be affected.

Yarn over between two knit stitches

STEP 1 Bring the yarn forward between the needles, then return it to the back of the work over the top of the right needle. The yarn is now wrapped from front to back around the right needle and in the correct position to knit the next stitch.

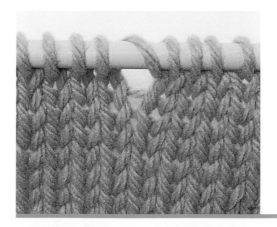

STEP 2 Knit the next stitch in the usual way and complete the row. This yarn over creates a hole between two knit stitches.

Yarn over between two purl stitches

STEP 1 Take the yarn to the back
of the work over the top of the right
needle, then bring it forward between the
needles. The yarn is now wrapped from
front to back around the right needle and
in the correct position to purl the next
stitch. This yarn over creates a hole
between two purl stitches.

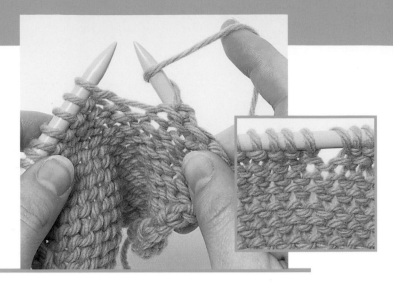

Yarn over after a knit stitch
and before a purl stitch

STEP 1 Bring the yarn forward
between the needles, then take it to the
back over the top of the right needle and
forward again between the needles. The
yarn is now in the correct position for
purling the next stitch. This yarn over
creates a hole between a knit stitch and a
purl stitch.

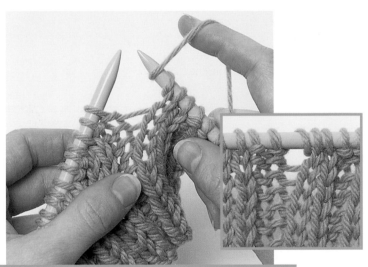

Yarn over after a purl stitch and
before a knit stitch

STEP 1 The yarn is in
the forward position after
working a purl stitch. Take
it to the back over the
top of the right needle.
Beware! If you take the
yarn back *between*
the needles you will
not create an
extra stitch.

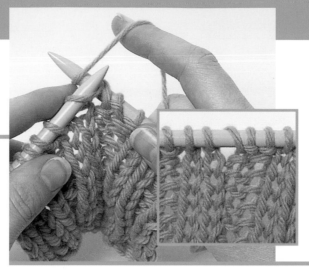

STEP 2 Knit the next stitch. This yarn over creates a hole between a purl stitch and a knit stitch.

MAKE ONE STITCH BY "LIFT AND KNIT" (ABBREVIATED **m1**)
A "lifted" eyelet increase is made by lifting up a strand of yarn from the row below and knitting it. This method makes a slightly smaller, neater hole than a yarn over.

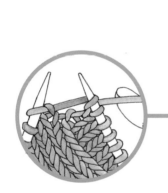

STEP 1 Insert the tip of the right needle under the horizontal strand of yarn between the last stitch worked and the next stitch.

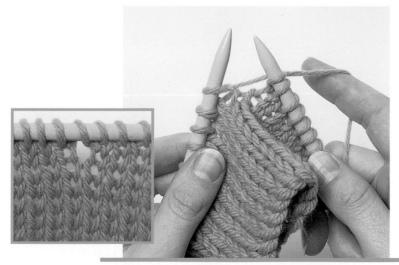

STEP 2 Wind the yarn knitwise around the right needle and pull a loop through, under the lifted strand, so knitting an extra stitch. The extra stitch creates a hole.

EXAMPLES OF LACE PATTERNS

The following stitch patterns show how the yarn over and "lifted" eyelets are used to form lacy textures. See page 127 for abbreviations.

Eyelet pattern 1 Each hole in this stitch pattern is made by a yarn over (**yo**—page 89), balanced by the "knit 2 together" (**k2tog**—page 67) that follows.

This pattern requires a multiple of 5 stitches.
Row 1 (RIGHT-SIDE ROW) K.
Row 2 P.
Row 3 K4, *yo, k2tog, k3, rep from * to last st, k1.
Row 4 P.
Row 5 K.
Row 6 P.
Row 7 K1, *yo, k2tog, k3, rep from * to last 4 sts, yo, k2tog, k2.
Row 8 P.
Repeat these 8 rows.

Eyelet pattern 2 In this example the holes are made by the "lift and knit" method (**m1**—page 91). Each extra stitch is balanced by the following "knit 2 together" (**k2tog**—page 67).

This pattern requires a multiple of 5 stitches, plus 3.
Row 1 (RIGHT-SIDE ROW) *K3, m1, k2tog, rep from * to last 3 sts, k3.
Row 2 P.
Row 3 K.
Row 4 P.
Repeat these 4 rows.

Zigzags On *row 1* of this pattern, each yarn over (**yo**—page 89) is balanced by the previous "knit 2 together" (**k2tog**—page 67), whereas on *row 3* each yarn over is balanced by the following "slip one, knit one, pass slipped stitch over" (**SKP**—pages 65–66). This alternation creates the zigzags.

This pattern requires a multiple of 5 stitches, plus 3.
Row 1 (RIGHT-SIDE ROW) K3, *k2tog, yo, k3, rep from * to end.
Row 2 P.
Row 3 K3, *yo, SKP, k3, rep from * to end.
Row 4 P.
Repeat these 4 rows.

Little towers This pattern uses the yarn over between two purl stitches (page 90). Each yarn over (**yo**—page 89) is balanced by the "purl 2 together" (**p2tog**—page 68) that follows.

This pattern requires a multiple of 6 stitches, plus 1.

Row 1 (RIGHT-SIDE ROW) P3, *yo, p2tog, p4, rep from * to last 4 sts, yo, p2tog, p2.

Row 2 K3, *p1 (into yo of previous row), k5, rep from * to last 4 sts, p1, k3.

Row 3 P3, *k1, p5, rep from * to last 4 sts, k1, p3.

Row 4 Repeat row 2.

Row 5 Repeat row 3.

Row 6 K.

Row 7 P6, *yo, p2tog, p4, rep from * to last st, p1.

Row 8 K6, *p1, k5, rep from * to last st, k1.

Row 9 P6, *k1, p5, rep from * to last st, p1.

Row 10 Repeat row 8.

Row 11 Repeat row 9.

Row 12 K.

Repeat these 12 rows.

Knotted lines This pattern uses the yarn over between two purl stitches (page 90). Each yarn over (**yo**—page 89) is balanced by the "purl 2 together" (**p2tog**—page 68) that follows it on *row 5* or precedes it on *row 7*.

This pattern requires a multiple of 2 stitches, plus 2.

Row 1 (RIGHT-SIDE ROW) K.

Row 2 P.

Row 3 K.

Row 4 P.

Row 5 P1, *yo, p2tog, rep from * to last st, p1.

Row 6 K.

Row 7 P1, *p2tog, yo, rep from * to last st, p1.

Row 8 P.

Repeat these 8 rows.

Chevrons In each repeat of this pattern four yarn overs are made, balanced by two single decreases (**SKP** and **k2tog**—pages 65–66 and 67) and one double decrease. These decreases are grouped together at the center of each repeat, which creates a wavy effect.

This pattern requires a multiple of 10 stitches, plus 1.

Row 1 (RIGHT-SIDE ROW) *[K1, yo] twice, SKP, sl 1, k2tog, pass sl st over, k2tog, yo, k1, yo, rep from * to last st, k1.

Row 2 P.

Repeat these 2 rows.

LADY'S LACY VEST

To wear by itself or over a T-shirt, this clever vest knits up very quickly on large needles. The dramatic zigzags are simply formed by the wide stitch pattern—very easy!—and emphasized by the unusual random dyed yarn, a cool, soft cotton tape.

SIZES

to fit bust	32	34	36	38	in.
	81	86	92	97	cm
actual measurement	36	38	40	42	in.
	92	97	102	107	cm
length to shoulder	19	19½	20	20½	in.
	48	49.5	51	52	cm

MATERIALS

COLINETTE YARNS WIGWAM (APPROX. 186 YDS/170 M PER 100 G HANK)

COLOR Monet (shade 101) 3[4 4 4] 100-g hanks

NEEDLES size 10½ (6½ mm)

GAUGE

If your gauge is correct over stockinette it will be correct over the zigzag pattern used. Required gauge over stockinette is 16 sts and 23 rows to 4 in. (10 cm). Using size 10½ (6½ mm) needles, cast on 20 sts and work 26 rows stockinette. Measure gauge (pages 50–51).

If your gauge is tight, with more sts or rows to 4 in. (10 cm), try another test piece with larger needles. If your gauge is loose, with fewer sts or rows to 4 in. (10 cm), try again with smaller needles.

NOTES

1. Instructions in brackets [ ] refer to the 3 larger sizes. Where only one set of figures is given this refers to all sizes.
2. Vest in photograph is 2nd size.

ABBREVIATIONS

k—knit; **p**—purl; **rep**—repeat; **st(s)**—stitch(es); **k2tog**—knit 2 together; **SKP**—slip one, knit one, pass slip stitch over; **SK2togpsso**—slip one, knit 2 together, pass slip stitch over, thus decreasing two stitches; **yo**—yarn over to make extra stitch (between two knit sts); **in.**—inches; **cm**—centimeters.

BACK

Using size 10½ (6½ mm) needles cast on 79[85, 91, 97] sts.

Rows 1 and 2 P to end.

Zigzag Pattern 1

Row 1 *K1, yo, k11[12, 13, 14], SK2togpsso, k11[12, 13, 14], yo, rep from * twice more to last st, k1.

Row 2 P to end.

Rep these 2 rows until Back measures 11½[12, 12, 12½] in./29[30.5, 31, 32] cm in all down to lower point, ending row 2. Make a note of the number of pattern rows you have worked.

Shape Armholes

Note that stitch pattern should remain constant throughout.

dec row 1 SKP, k10[11, 12, 13], SK2togpsso, place a ring marker on this st, pattern as established ending SK2togpsso, k10[11, 12, 13], k2tog.

dec row 2 P to end.

dec row 3 SKP, k to 1 st before marker, pattern as established (begin SK2togpsso) to last 2 sts, k2tog.

dec row 4 P to end.

Rep dec rows 3 and 4, 3[4, 4, 5] more times.

1st and 3rd sizes only

Next row SKP, pattern as established (begin SK2togpsso), ending SK2togpsso, k2tog.

2nd and 4th sizes only
Next row SKP, k2tog, pattern as established ending SKP, k2tog.
All Sizes
Next row P to end. 55[59, 63, 67] sts. **
Zigzag Pattern 2
1st row K1, k2tog, *k11[12, 13, 14], yo, k1, yo, k11[12, 13, 14], *SK2togpsso, rep from * to * once more, SKP, k1.
2nd row P to end.
Rep these 2 rows until Back measures 19[19½, 20, 20½] in./48[49.5, 51, 52] cm in all down to lower point, ending 2nd row.
Bind off. Cut yarn leaving a short tail. Make a note of the total number of pattern rows.

FRONT
Work as given for Back to **.
Shape Front Neck: First Side
1st row K1, k2tog, k11[12, 13, 14], yo, k2, turn. Work on these sts only:
2nd row P to end.
Rep these 2 rows until length matches Back ending 2nd row. Bind off leaving a 10 in. (25 cm) tail.
Second Side
With right side of Front facing, rejoin yarn at right of remaining sts. Bind off 23[25, 27, 29] sts at center. 16[17, 18, 19] sts remain.
1st row K2, yo, k11[12, 13, 14], SKP, k1.
2nd row P to end.
Rep these 2 rows until length matches Back ending 2nd row. Bind off leaving a 10 in. (25 cm) tail.

ASSEMBLY
Block pieces using water-spray method (page 41). Join left shoulder seam with backstitch (pages 44–45) using tail left for this purpose, matching pattern.

NECK BORDER
With right side of work facing, using size 10½ (6½ mm) needles, begin at top of back neck in 2nd yo along top edge: pick up and k25[27, 29, 31] sts, ending in next yo; 18[18, 20, 20] sts down first side of front neck shaping; 23[25, 27, 29] sts from center front and 18[18, 20, 20] sts

from second side of front neck shaping. 84[88, 96, 100] sts.
Next row K to end. Bind off.
Join remaining shoulder seam, matching pattern.

ARMHOLE EDGE MAKE 2
With right side of work facing, using size 10½ (6½ mm) needles, pick up and k64[64, 68, 68] sts evenly from armhole edge.
Next row K to end. Bind off.
Using mattress stitch (pages 42–43) join side seams, matching patterns. Run in yarn ends along seams.

TIP
If the colors of a space-dyed yarn coincide, producing a pattern you don't like as the knitting proceeds, cut yarn and rejoin leaving approx. 8 in. (20 cm) tails, to break the rhythm; or join in a 2nd ball and work in stripes of 2 rows from each ball.

CABLES AND TWISTS

Different arrangements of cables and twists, crossed from right to left or from left to right, give rise to many interesting stitch patterns, such as those used in traditional Aran knitting.

CABLES

These are formed by crossing one group of stitches over another at regular intervals such as every four, six, or eight rows. Each group may be two, three, or more stitches. A cable of two groups of two stitches is called a four-stitch cable. The examples below are six-stitch cables, worked with two groups of three stitches. Cables are worked with the help of a cable needle: a short double-pointed needle, about 4 in. (10 cm) long (see page 15). This may be straight or shaped with a kink in the middle to prevent stitches from slipping off. Choose a cable needle slightly smaller in size than the main needles in use, to avoid stretching the stitches.

Cable to left (six-stitch cable shown, abbreviated **C6L**)

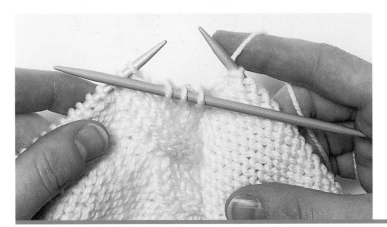

STEP 1 On a right-side row, work to the position required for the cable. Holding the cable needle at the front of the work, insert it purlwise into the first group (three stitches), slipping them one by one off the left needle.

STEP 2 Keeping the cable needle at the front of the work, knit the next group (next 3 stitches).

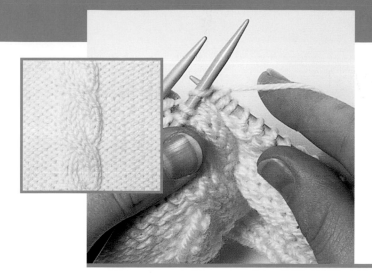

STEP 3 Then knit the group of stitches on the cable needle, beginning with the first stitch slipped. The cable twists to the left. The cable shown here was worked on every eighth row.

Cable to right
(six-stitch cable shown, abbreviated **C6R**)

STEP 1 On a right-side row, work to the position required for the cable. Holding the cable needle at the back of the work, insert it purlwise into the first group (three stitches), slipping them one by one off the left needle.

STEP 2 Keeping the cable needle at the back of the work, knit the next group (next three stitches). Then knit the group of stitches on the cable needle, beginning with the first stitch slipped. The cable twists to the right. The cable shown here was worked on every eighth row.

TWISTS

These are simply two stitches worked in such a way as to twist either to the right or the left. No cable needle is necessary.

Left twist (abbreviated **LT**)

STEP 1

On a right-side row, work to the required position. Skip the first stitch on the left needle and insert the right needle into the back of the second stitch, behind the first stitch. Wrap the yarn knitwise and pull through a loop, leaving the second stitch on the left needle.

STEP 2

Insert the right needle through the back loops of the first and second stitches together, wrap the yarn knitwise, and pull through another loop, slipping both stitches off the left needle.

Moving the position of the left twist by one stitch to the left on every right-side row creates a diagonal line sloping up to the left.

TIP

To make a Left Twist that is the exact reverse of the Right Twist on page 99, it is necessary to insert the right needle from the back of the work (behind the first stitch) into the *front* of the second stitch instead of the back.

Right twist
(abbreviated **RT**)

STEP 1
On a right-side row, work to the required position. Insert the right needle knitwise into the first two stitches together. Wrap the yarn knitwise and pull through a loop, leaving both stitches on the left needle.

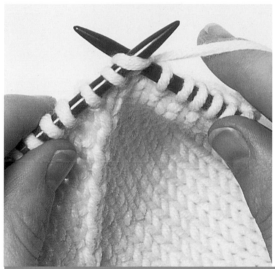

STEP 2
Knit the first stitch again in the usual way.

STEP 3
Slip both stitches off the left needle.

Moving the position of the right twist by one stitch to the right on every right-side row creates a diagonal line sloping up to the right.

EXAMPLES OF CABLE AND TWIST PATTERNS

Special abbreviations used: **C4R**—cable 4 sts to right thus: slip next 2 sts onto cable needle at back of work, k next 2 sts then k2 from cable needle; **C4L**—cable 4 sts to left, as C4R but holding cable needle at front of work; **RT**—right twist; **LT**—left twist

◄ **Double cable panel** Shown here worked over 8 sts (2 cables, each of 4 sts), with 1 st at each side in reverse stockinette stitch, making a panel 10 sts wide on a background of stockinette stitch.

Work the required 10 sts as follows, with the remaining sts in stockinette stitch:

Row 1 (RIGHT-SIDE ROW) P1, k8, p1.
Row 2 K1, p8, k1.
Rows 3 AND 4 Repeat rows 1 and 2.
Row 5 P1, C4R, C4L, p1.
Row 6 Repeat row 2.
Repeat these 6 rows.

▲ **Zigzags** requires a multiple of 5 sts, plus 2.

Row 1 (RIGHT-SIDE ROW) K1, *LT, k3, repeat from * to last st, k1.
ROW 2 AND EVERY WRONG-SIDE ROW P.
Row 3 K2, *LT, k3, repeat from * to end.
Row 5 K3, *LT, k3, repeat from * to last 4 sts, LT, k2.
Row 7 K1, *k3, LT, repeat from * to last st, k1.
Row 9 K1, *k3, RT, repeat from * to last st, k1.
Row 11 K3, *RT, k3, repeat from * to last 4 sts, rt, k2.
Row 13 K2, *RT, k3, repeat from * to end.
Row 15 K1, *RT, k3, repeat from * to last st, k1.
Row 16 P.
Repeat these 16 rows.

▼ **Honeycomb pattern** requires a multiple of 8 sts.

Row 1 (RIGHT-SIDE ROW) K.
Row 2 P.
Row 3 *C4L, C4R, repeat from * to end.
Row 4 P.
Row 5 AND 6 Repeat rows 1 and 2.
Row 7 *C4R, C4L, repeat from * to end.
Row 8 P.
Repeat these 8 rows.

▲ **Raindrops** requires a multiple of 5 sts, plus 1.

Row 1 (RIGHT-SIDE ROW) K3, *RT, k3, repeat from * to last 3 sts, RT, k1.
ROW 2 AND EVERY WRONG SIDE ROW P.
Row 3 K2, *RT, k3, repeat from * to last 4 sts, RT, k2.
Row 5 K1, *RT, k3, repeat from * to end.
ROWS 7 AND 9 K.
Row 10 P.
Repeat these 10 rows.

TEXTURED STITCHES

There are several different ways in which stitches may be worked: long stitches, slipped stitches, yarn overs, reversed stitches, and increases or decreases can all be combined in many different ways to form a huge variety of patterns. Long stitches and slip stitches are described below; the other techniques used for the stitch patterns in this section are described elsewhere: yarn overs on pages 89–90, reverse stitches on page 37, and increases and decreases on pages 62–70.

LONG STITCH
Formed by wrapping the yarn two (or more) times around the needle instead of once, and dropping the extra loop(s) on the following row. Shown here worked knitwise, winding the yarn twice around the needle (abbreviated **kwtw**).

STEP 1 Insert the right needle knitwise in the required stitch and wrap the yarn twice around the needle tip, instead of once.

STEP 2 Pull the double loop through in the same way as when knitting a stitch.

STEP 3

On the following row, the double loop may be worked as knit or purl, according to the pattern; here the right needle is shown inserted knitwise. Work the stitch and drop the extra loop from the needle.

A complete row of long stitches, worked as part of a long stitch stripe pattern of five rows of garter stitch (knit every row) followed by one row of long stitches (repeat these 6 rows).

Slip stitches Long stitches, and other stitches, may be slipped from one row to the next without working into them. To prevent twisting, such stitches should always be slipped purlwise, unless directed otherwise. Depending on the pattern row, the working yarn may be held behind or in front of the slip stitch.

Slip one with yarn in back (abbreviated **sl 1 wyib**) Normally worked on a right-side row, to keep the slip stitch at the right side of the work. With the yarn at the side of work away from you (as when working a knit stitch), insert the right needle purlwise into the required stitch and slip it from the left needle to the right needle without working into it.

Slip one with yarn in front (abbreviated **sl 1 wyif**) Normally worked on a wrong side row, to keep the slip stitch at the right side of the work. With the yarn at the side of work nearest to you (as when working a purl stitch), insert the right needle purlwise into the required stitch and slip it from the left needle to the right needle without working into it.

EXAMPLES OF TEXTURED STITCH PATTERNS
Special abbreviations used: kwtw—knit winding yarn twice; **pwtw**—purl winding yarn twice; **sl 1**—slip one (purlwise); **wyib**—with yarn in back; **wyif**—with yarn in front; **p3tog**—purl 3 together; **MB**—make bobble thus: k into front, back and front again of next st, turn the work, p3, turn the work, k3, pass first and second sts over third st; **MT**—make tail thus: turn the work and using the two-needle method (see pages 20–23), cast on 5 sts onto the left needle, bind off the same 5 sts, slip 1 st from the right needle to the left needle, turn the work, and push the tail to the right side of the work before continuing along the row.

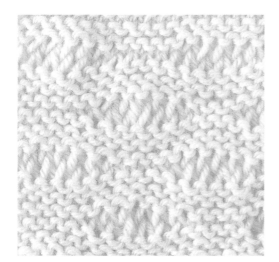

Long stitch waves requires a multiple of 10 sts, plus 9.

Row 1 TO 3 K.
Row 4 K2, *(kwtw) 5 times, k5, repeat from * to last 7 sts, (kwtw) 5 times, k2.
Row 5 K2, *(kwtw dropping extra loop) 5 times, k5, repeat from * to last 7 sts, (kwtw dropping extra loop) 5 times, k2.
Row 6 K2, *(k1 dropping extra loop) 5 times, k5, repeat from * to last 7 sts, (k1 dropping extra loop) 5 times, k2.
Row 7 TO 9 K.
Row 10 K2, *k5, (kwtw) 5 times, repeat from * to last 7 sts, k7.
Row 11 K2, *k5, (kwtw dropping extra loop) 5 times, repeat from * to last 7 sts, k7.
Row 12 K2, *k5, (k1 dropping extra loop) 5 times, repeat from * to last 7 sts, k7.
Repeat these 12 rows.

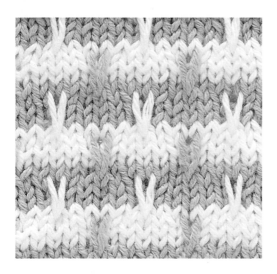

Slip stitch bricks requires a multiple of 6 sts, plus 3.

In this slip stitch pattern, long stitches are slipped for 3 rows before being worked.
Row 1 (RIGHT-SIDE ROW) Using first color, knit.
Row 2 P1, *pwtw, p5, repeat from * to last 2 sts, pwtw, p1.
Row 3 Change to second color, k1, *sl 1 wyib dropping extra loop, k5, repeat from * to last 2 sts, sl 1 wyib dropping extra loop, k1.
Row 4 P1, *sl 1 wyif, p5, repeat from * to last 2 sts, sl 1 wyif, p1.
Row 5 K1, *sl 1 wyib, k5, repeat from * to last 2 sts, sl 1 wyib, k1.
Row 6 P4, *pwtw, p5, repeat from * to last 5 sts, pwtw, p4.
Row 7 Change to first color, k4, *sl 1 wyib dropping extra loop, k5, repeat from * to last 5 sts, sl 1 wyib dropping extra loop, k4.
Row 8 P4, *sl 1 wyif, p5, repeat from * to last 5 sts, sl 1 wyif, p4.
Row 9 K4, *sl 1 wyib, k5, repeat from * to last 5 sts, sl 1 wyib, k4.
Row 10 P1, *pwtw, p5, repeat from * to last 2 sts, pwtw, p1.
Repeat rows 3 to 10, ending with either row 5 or 9.
Finish by purling one row.

Trinity stitch requires a multiple of 4 sts.

Row 1 (RIGHT-SIDE ROW) P.
Row 2 *(K1, p1, k1) all into same stitch, p3tog, repeat from * to end.
Row 3 P.
Row 4 *P3tog, (k1, p1, k1) all into same stitch, repeat from * to end.
Repeat these 4 rows.

Bobble dots requires a multiple of 6 sts, plus 3.

Row 1 (RIGHT-SIDE ROW) K.
Row 2 P.
Row 3 K1, *MB, k5, repeat from * to last 2 sts, MB, k1.
Row 4 Purl, pushing bobbles to front of work.
Row 5 TO 8 Repeat rows 1 and 2, twice.
Row 9 K4, *MB, k5, repeat from * to last 5 sts, MB, k4.
Row 10 Repeat row 4.
Rows 11 AND 12 Repeat rows 1 and 2.
Repeat these 12 rows.

Little tails requires a multiple of 6 sts, plus 3.

Row 1 (RIGHT-SIDE ROW) K.
Row 2 P.
Row 3 K1, *MT, k5, repeat from * to last 2 sts, MT, k1.
Row 4 Purl, pushing tails to right side of work.
Row 5 AND 6 Repeat rows 1 and 2.
Row 7 K4, *MT, k5, repeat from * to last 5 sts, MT, k4.
Row 8 Repeat row 4.
Repeat these 8 rows.

CABLE CUSHION

Practice your cabling skills with this tactile cushion, textured with Plaited Cables and Twists. In Aran-weight yarn, it's quick to knit, with no shaping to distract you from the pattern. You might want two or three!

FINISHED SIZE
to fit pillow form   16 x 16 in. (40 x 40 cm)

MATERIALS
KING COLE MOBY 100 (APPROX. 210 YDS/192 M PER 100 G BALL)
COLOR granary (shade 89) 2 100-g balls
NEEDLES sizes 7 (4½ mm) and 6 (4 mm)
cable needle
3 large buttons

GAUGE
Using size 7 (4½ mm) needles, cast on 29 sts and work 26 rows Cable Pattern as below. This piece should easily stretch to a width of 6 in. (15 cm), as it will be stretched in use, and length should measure 4 in. (10 cm). If your test-piece is too small, try another with larger needles. If your test-piece is too large, try again with smaller needles.

Gauge is not crucial provided a change in size is acceptable, but if your gauge is too loose extra yarn may be required and the cushion cover will stretch in use.

ABBREVIATIONS
k—knit; **p**—purl; **rep**—repeat; **st(s)**—stitch(es); **C6R**—cable 6 sts to right: slip 3 sts to cable needle, hold at back of work, k next 3 sts then k3 from cable needle; **C6L**—cable 6 sts to left: as C6R but hold cable needle at front of work; **RT**—right twist; **in.**—inches; **cm**—centimeters.

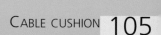

CUSHION

Using size 6 (4 mm) needles cast on 71 sts.

Button Band

Rib row 1 *K1, p1, rep from * to last st, k1.

Rib row 2 *P1, k1, rep from * to last st, p1.

Rep these 2 rows 4 more times. 10 rib rows in all.

Change to size 7 (4½ mm) needles.

Cable Pattern

Row 1 K1, *RT, p2, RT, p3, k9, p3, rep from * to last 7 sts, RT, p2, RT, k1.

Row 2 K1, *p2, k2, p2, k3, p9, k3, rep from * to last 7 sts, p2, k2, p2, k1.

Rows 3 and 4 Rep rows 1 and 2

Row 5 K1, *RT, p2, RT, p3, C6R, k3, p3, rep from * to last 7 sts, RT, p2, RT, k1.

Row 6 Rep row 2

Rows 7–10 Rep rows 1 and 2, twice in all

Row 11 K1, *RT, p2, RT, p3, k3, C6L, p3, rep from * to last 7 sts, RT, p2, RT, k1.

Row 12 Rep row 2

Rep these 12 rows until piece measures 30 in. (76 cm) ending with row 2 or row 8.

Change to size 6 (4 mm) needles.

Buttonhole Band

Rep rib rows 1 and 2 as for Button Band, twice in all. See Two-Row Buttonhole (page 83).

5th row rib 13 sts as established, *bind off next 3 sts, 1 st remains on right needle, rib next 17 sts as established, rep from * once more, bind off next 3 sts, rib as established to end. 3 buttonholes.

6th row *rib as established to buttonhole, turn work, cast on 3 sts, turn work, rep from * twice more, rib as established to end.

Rep rib rows 1 and 2 as for Button Band, twice more. 10 rib rows in all.

Bind off in k and p as established. Cut yarn leaving a 4 in. (10 cm) tail.

ASSEMBLY

Do not block or press.

With right side outwards, fold work to form a square with Buttonhole Band overlapping Button Band at center back. Use mattress stitch (pages 42–43) to join side edges. Run in remaining yarn ends.

Sew on buttons to match buttonholes.

TIP

You can easily see the stitches in this pattern because the cables and twists form strong vertical lines. But it's not so easy to keep count of the rows: write the row numbers 1–12 on a scrap of paper and check off each row as you complete it, over and over until your work is the required length. Then you won't work the cables on the wrong row!

FAIR ISLE (TWO-COLOR KNITTING)

Fair Isle knitting derives from the multi-colored traditional knitting of the Shetland Isles, worked in stockinette stitch in many colors, but never with more than two colors in one row. Traditional patterns consisted of small motifs repeated across the work and were often worked "in the round" so that the right side of the pattern was always visible. The term "Fair Isle" is nowadays used to describe any multi-colored knitting with a pattern repeat. To work such a pattern, the color not in use must be carried across the wrong side of the work by one of the methods described below.

STRANDING

Use this method to carry a color across the wrong side of no more than four stitches. For longer intervals, use the twisting technique on page 109.

Each strand of yarn left on the wrong side of the work is called a "float." Long floats tend to catch on fingers or jewelry and so the knitting can be spoiled. Short floats are fine. Do not work too tightly or the knitting will be distorted. The floats should be loose enough to allow the knitting to lie completely flat. When stranding or twisting, some knitters find it convenient to hold the main color in the right hand in the usual way, and the contrast color with the fingers of the left hand. This method avoids the need to drop the colors and pick them up again but needs practice to achieve an even gauge.

STRANDING ON A KNIT ROW

STEP 1 At the position required for a stitch in the contrast color (orange), insert the right needle into the next stitch, drop the main color (blue) from the right forefinger and pick up the contrast color *in front* of the main color. Use the contrast to knit the required stitches to the position of the next color change.

STEP 2

Insert the right needle into the next stitch, drop the contrast color (orange) from the right forefinger and pick up the main color *behind* the contrast color. Use the main color to knit the required stitches to the position of the next color change. Repeat steps 1 and 2 as required to the end of the row.

STRANDING ON A PURL ROW
Pick up and drop the main and contrast colors in the same way without twisting them, keeping one color always above the other. The color carried lower will be slightly more prominent on the right side of the work, so if the colors are not carried consistently throughout, the surface will appear uneven.

TIP
Spread out the stitches on the right needle when changing colors to prevent the floats from becoming too short and puckering the work.

AT THE BEGINNING OF A KNIT OR PURL ROW
Fair Isle patterns are often worked with a selvage stitch in the main color at each edge. At the beginning of every row (shown here on a knit row), twist the contrast color around the main color before using the main color for the selvage stitch. This keeps the edge stitches neat.

TWISTING

Where a pattern requires one color to pass behind more than four stitches of another color, the yarns should be twisted every two or three stitches on the wrong side of the work.

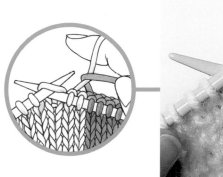

TWISTING ON A KNIT ROW
At the position required for a twist, drop the color in use (white), pass the other color (blue) over it, and pick up the color in use (white) again with the right forefinger. At the next position for a twist, drop the color in use, pass the other color under it, and pick up the color in use. Alternating the direction of the twists in this way prevents the yarns from becoming tangled.

TWISTING ON A PURL ROW
Twist the two colors in the same way, every two or three stitches.

TIP
If you've finished a garment and suddenly spot a small mistake in a Fair Isle pattern, it is possible to cheat a little (unless you are a true perfectionist) by using swiss darning to change the color of one or two stitches, as shown on page 118.

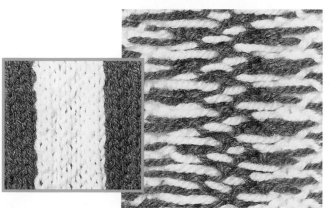

Stagger the position of the twists from row to row to prevent the twists from showing through on the right side of the work.

AT THE BEGINNING OF A KNIT OR PURL ROW
Twist the colors together in the same way as when stranding.

PROJECT 9
FAIR ISLE SWEATER

With a boldly patterned front, plain back, and plain sleeves, this young design knits up quickly in Aran wool yarn. The coordinating shoulder bag completes the look—if you're new to Fair Isle knitting, try making the bag before tackling the sweater.

SIZES
SWEATER

to fit bust	32	34	36	38	in.
	81	86	92	97	cm
actual measurement	36	38½	41	43½	in.
	92	98	104	110.5	cm
length to shoulder	19½	20	21	21½	in.
	49.5	51	53.5	54.5	cm
sleeve seam	17	17½	17½	18	in.
	43	44.5	44.5	46	cm

BAG
10 x 10 in. (25 x 25 cm)

MATERIALS (SWEATER)
JAEGER MATCHMAKER MERINO ARAN (APPROX. 90 YDS/82 M PER 50 G BALL)

COLOR A soft camel (shade 766) 8[9 10 11] 50-g balls

COLOR B mariner (shade 629) 1 50-g ball

COLOR C sage (shade 755) 1 50-g ball

COLOR D glow (shade 762) 1 50-g ball

COLOR E rosy (shade 764) 1 50-g ball

COLOR F cream (shade 662) 1 50-g ball

NEEDLES sizes 8 (5 mm), 7 (4½ mm), and 5 (3¾ mm)

set of 4 double-pointed or circular needle size 6 (4 mm)

2 stitch holders

MATERIALS (BAG)
COLOR A soft camel (shade 766) 2 50-g balls, plus remnants of contrast colors from Sweater

pairs of needles as for Sweater

zipper length 10 in. (25 cm) to match col.A

GAUGE
Required gauge over stockinette is 19 sts and 25 rows to 4 in. (10 cm). Using size 7 (4½ mm) needles, cast on 25 sts and work 28 rows stockinette. Measure gauge (pages 50–51).

If your gauge is tight, with more sts or rows to 4 in. (10 cm), try another test-piece with larger needles. If your gauge is loose, with fewer sts or rows to 4 in. (10 cm), try again with smaller needles. Required gauge over Fair Isle pattern is 19 sts and 23 rows to 4 in. (10 cm); you will probably need needles one size larger than those for stockinette, i.e. size 8 (5 mm). Cast on 25 sts and work 30 rows Fair Isle Pattern as below. Measure gauge and adjust needle size if necessary.

ABBREVIATIONS
k—knit; p—purl; rep—repeat; st(s)—stitch(es); inc—increase; k2tog—knit 2 together; SKP—slip one, knit one, pass slip stitch over; p2tog—purl 2 together; kfb—knit into front and back of same stitch; m1 tbl—make one through back loop; sl 1 wyif—slip 1 with yarn in front; col.—color; in.—inches; cm—centimeters.

NOTES
1. Instructions in brackets [ ] refer to the 3 larger sizes. Where only one set of figures is given this refers to all sizes.
2. Sweater in photograph is 2nd size.

FRONT

Using size 5 (3¾ mm) needles and col.A cast on 85[91, 97, 103] sts.

Rib row 1 *P1, k2, rep from * to last st, p1.

Rib row 2 *K1, p2, rep from * to last st, k1.

Rep these 2 rows until rib measures 2[2, 2½, 3] in./5[5, 6.5, 7.5]cm ending rib row 1 (right-side row).

Change to size 7 (4½ mm) needles and col.B.

Next row Kfb, p to last st, kfb. 87[93, 99, 105] sts. ** Cut col.A.

Fair Isle Pattern (see chart on page 112)

NOTE: cols. should be twisted or stranded (pages 107–109) on every 2-color row. When cutting and joining in cols. leave 4 in. (10 cm) tails to be run in later.

Change to size 8 (5 mm) needles if necessary.

Row 1 (right-side row) Join in cols. B and C. In cols. as shown reading chart row 1 from right to left, k first st, k next 6 sts 14[15, 16, 17] times, k last 2 sts.

Row 2 (wrong-side row) Reading chart row 2 from left to right, p 1st and 2nd sts, p next 6 sts 14[15, 16, 17] times, p last st.

Continue in this way, reading from successive chart rows, cutting and joining in cols. as necessary, until chart row 40 is complete.

Work chart rows 1–20 again. 60 Fair Isle rows. Total length (including ribbing) should measure 12[12, 12½, 13] in./30.5[30.5, 32, 33] cm.

Shape Armholes

Keeping pattern constant, beginning chart row 21, bind off 6 sts at beginning next 2 rows (knitwise on right-side row, purlwise on wrong-side row).

dec row 1 SKP, pattern as established to last 2 sts, k2tog.

dec row 2 pattern as established.

Rep these 2 rows 5[5, 8, 8] more times, ending chart row 34[34, 40, 40]. 63[69, 69, 75] sts.

1st and 2nd Sizes Only

Work chart rows 35–40 as established.

All Sizes

Change to size 7 (4½ mm) needles and col.A, k 1 row. Change to col.C, p 1 row. Change to col.D, k 1 row. Change to col. E, p 1 row. Change to col.A and continue in stockinette until Front measures 5[5½, 6, 6] in./

12.5[14, 15, 15] cm from beginning of armhole shaping, ending p row.

Shape Neck: First Side

Neck row 1 K 25[27, 27, 29] sts, turn. Work on these sts only:

Neck row 2 P2tog, p to last st, k1.

Neck row 3 K to last 2 sts, k2tog.

Rep neck rows 2 and 3, 3 more times.17[19, 19, 21] sts remain.

Continue in stockinette until Front measures 7½ [8, 8½, 8½] in./19[20.5, 21.5, 21.5] cm from beginning of armhole shaping, ending p row. Total length 19½ [20, 21, 21½] in./49.5[51, 53.5, 54.5] cm.

Shape Shoulder

Bind off 8[9, 9, 10] sts at beginning next row, k to end. Work 1 p row. Bind off remaining 9[10, 10, 11] sts.

Second Side

With right side of Front facing, slip 13[15, 15, 17] sts at center front to a holder. Rejoin col.A at right of remaining sts and k 25[27, 27, 29] sts to end.

Neck row 2 K1, p to last 2 sts, p2tog tbl.

Neck row 3 SKP, k to end.

Rep these 2 rows, 3 more times. 17[19, 19, 21] sts remain.

Continue in stockinette until length matches First Side at beginning of shoulder shaping, ending p row.

K 1 row.

Shape Shoulder

Bind off 8[9, 9, 10] sts purlwise at beginning next row, P to end. Work 1 k row. Bind off remaining 9[10, 10, 11] sts purlwise.

Run in all Fair Isle ends along wrong side of rows (page 45).

BACK

Work as given for Front to **.

Continue in stockinette and col.A, beginning with a k row, until length matches Front at beginning of armhole shaping, ending with a p row. NOTE: there will be a few more rows than on Front, not the same number.

Shape Armholes

Bind off 6 sts at beginning next 2 rows (knitwise on right-side row, purlwise on wrong-side row).

dec row 1 SKP, k to last 2 sts, k2tog.

dec row 2 P.

Rep these 2 rows 5[5, 8, 8] more times. 63[69, 69, 75] sts.

Continue in stockinette until length matches Front at beginning of shoulder shaping, ending p row.

Shape Shoulders

Bind off 8[9, 9, 10] sts at beginning next 2 rows, and 9[10, 10, 11] sts at beginning following 2 rows (knitwise on right-side rows, purlwise on wrong-side rows).

Leave remaining 29[31, 31, 33] sts on a holder.

SLEEVES MAKE 2

Using size 5 (3¾ mm) needles and col.A cast on 43[43, 46, 46] sts.

Rep rib rows 1 and 2 as for Front, 8 times in all. 16 rib rows.

Change to size 7 (4½ mm) needles.

Shape Sleeve

Row 1 K1, m1 tbl, k to last st, m1 tbl, k1. 45[45, 48, 48] sts.

Work 5 rows stockinette, beginning and ending p row.

Rep these 6 rows 12[12, 14, 14] more times. 69[69, 76, 76] sts.

Continue in stockinette until Sleeve measures 17[17½, 17½, 18] in./43[44.5, 44.5, 46] cm in all, or length required, ending with a p row.

Shape Top of Sleeve

Cast off 6 sts at beginning next 2 rows (knitwise on right-side row, purlwise on wrong-side row). 57[57, 64, 64] sts remain.

Rep dec rows 1 and 2 as for Back, 12[12, 15, 15] times in all. 33[33, 34, 34] sts remain.

Next row SKP, k to last 2 sts, k2tog.

Following row P2tog, p to last 2 sts, p2tog tbl. 29[29, 30, 30] sts remain.

Rep these 2 rows once more. Bind off remaining 25[25, 26, 26] sts.

TURTLENECK

Block Front and Back using warm-steam method (page 41), avoiding ribbing. Join shoulder seams using backstitch (page 44). With right side of work facing, using set of 4 double-pointed or circular needle size 6 (4 mm) and col.A, begin at right shoulder seam, k across 29[31, 31, 33] sts

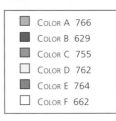

from holder at back neck, pick up and k (pages 46–47) 24[25, 28, 29] sts from first side of front neck shaping, k across 13[15, 15, 17] sts from holder at center front and pick up and k24 [25, 28, 29] sts from second side of front neck shaping. 90[96, 102, 108] sts. Work in rounds with wrong side of turtleneck facing you:

Round 1 *P2, k1, rep from * to end.

Rep this round until turtleneck measures 6 in. (15 cm), ending at right shoulder seam. Change to a size 7 (4½ mm) needle and bind off in k and p as established.

ASSEMBLY

Block Sleeves using warm-steam method (page 41), avoiding ribbing. Fold one Sleeve in half to find center of top edge. Matching this point to shoulder seam, join top edge of Sleeve to armhole (page 44). Sew on other Sleeve in same way. Join side and sleeve seams using mattress stitch (pages 42–43). Press seams using warm steam, avoiding ribbing. Fold turtleneck over.

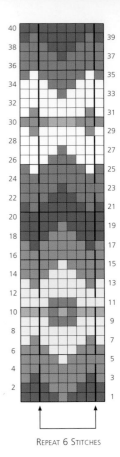

	COLOR A 766
	COLOR B 629
	COLOR C 755
	COLOR D 762
	COLOR E 764
	COLOR F 662

REPEAT 6 STITCHES

BAG

Front Panel

Using size 7 (4½ mm) needles and col.A, cast on 51 sts.

Beginning with a p row, work 16 rows stockinette, ending with a k row.

Change to col.E, p1 row. Change to col.D, k1 row. Change to col.C, p1 row.

Change to col.A, k1 row. 20 rows in all.

Fair Isle Pattern

Change to size 8 (5 mm) needles. Work in Fair Isle Pattern as given for Sweater Front, but beginning chart row 21 and ending chart row 40, and repeating the 6 sts 8 times. 20 pattern rows; 40 rows in all.

Change to size 7 (4½ mm) needles and col.A, k1 row. Change to col.C, p1 row. Change to col.D, k1 row. Change to col.E, p1 row.

Change to col.A and work 16 rows stockinette, beginning k row and ending p row. 60 rows in all.

Fold row (right-side row) p to end.

Back Panel

Continue in stockinette, beginning with a p row, until Back length matches Front exactly when piece is folded along fold row. NOTE: there will be a few more rows than Front Panel. End with a p row.

Bind off.

STRAP

Using size 5 (3¾ mm) needles and col.A, cast on 9 sts.

Row 1 sl 1 purlwise wyif, k8.

Rep this row until Strap measures 32 in. (81 cm) when slightly stretched (as it will be in use). Bind off.

ASSEMBLY

Block Bag using warm-steam method (page 41). Set zipper between cast-on and bound-off edges, back-stitching in place (page 85). Join side seams. Sew one end of Strap to top left corner of Front Panel and other end to opposite corner of Back Panel.

TIPS

1. The bag strap is made with a chain stitch selvage on both edges (page 59).

2. For a really neat finish, work all the other pieces with simple garter stitch selvage (page 59): on every wrong-side row of stockinette and Fair Isle pattern, work the first and last st as k instead of p. When assembling, take these selvage sts into seams.

INTARSIA (PICTURE KNITTING)

This technique is used for knitting blocks of separate colors without carrying yarns across the wrong side of the work. A separate ball of yarn is wound for each area of color. Intarsia knitting is therefore suitable for large geometric designs and picture knitting. It is normally worked from a chart.

ORGANIZING THE YARN

You need a separate ball of yarn for each area of color: some balls may need to be wound into two or more small balls.

Larger balls of yarn may be kept clean and tidy by placing them in plastic bags loosely secured with rubber bands. Small amounts of yarn may be wound onto bobbins which may be purchased or homemade. You can make your own bobbins by tracing the outline of Fig 1 onto cardboard and cutting it out. Wind the yarn round the bobbin as shown in Fig 2.

FIG 1

FIG 2

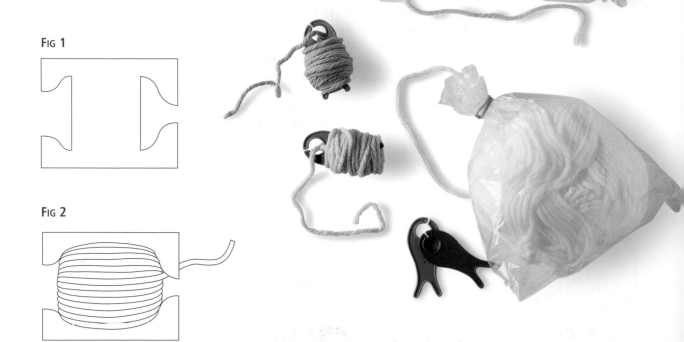

READING FROM A CHART

Each small square, or rectangle, on a chart represents one stitch, and a chart normally shows the knit side of stockinette stitch. Charts may be printed in color, or each area may be labeled with a color name or each stitch square may contain a symbol for a particular color.

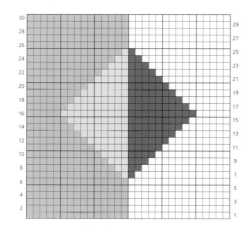

A chart may show the whole width of the knitting, with the different sizes indicated by dotted lines, or it may show only the area of a motif, when the stitches at each side of the motif are in one background color.

Rows are usually numbered on the side edges of the chart, with odd numbers (right-side rows) numbered at the right and even numbers (wrong-side rows) at the left.

Working in stockinette stitch, read knit rows (right-side rows with odd numbers) from right to left, and purl rows (wrong-side rows with even numbers) from left to right. Count the stitches carefully.

1. FIRST ROW OF THE MOTIF
Use the first color to knit the required number of stitches. Drop the first color, pick up the second color, and leaving a 6 in. (15 cm) tail, use it to knit the required number of stitches. The tail will be run in later, tightening the first stitch. Continue in this way along the row, using as many different balls of yarn as the design requires. If there are two areas of the same color, use a separate ball for each area. If you carry a color across from one area to another, the result will be uneven.

2. SUBSEQUENT ROWS
Colors are twisted around each other at each color change to avoid holes in the work.

To change colors on a knit row At the position required for a color change, drop the old color and pick up the new color behind the previous color, so that the yarns are crossed on the wrong side of the work. Work the first stitch in the new color rather tightly.

To change colors on a purl row Bring the new color up behind the previous color in the same way so the yarns are crossed on the wrong side of the work (the side facing you).

Here is the right side of the work.

3. RUN IN THE ENDS

At the end of each color area, cut the color no longer required, leaving a 6 in. (15 cm) tail. Leave all the tails at the wrong side of the work.

Thread each tail into a blunt-tipped needle. On the wrong side, begin by passing the needle up through the top loop of the adjoining stitch of another color (not the adjoining stitch of the same color) and pull gently to tighten the first (or last) stitch to the correct size.

Then thread the needle in and out of the loops along the edge of the color block for at least 2 in. (5 cm) before cutting the tail.

TIPS

1. Check off each row of the chart as you complete it.
2. If your chart is not in color, tape a small piece of each color to the chart key to avoid mistakes.
3. Untangle the balls and bobbins every few rows.
4. When working a color change several stitches along the row from the previous change, twist the colors every one or two stitches in the same way as for Fair Isle knitting (pages 107–109) to carry the new color into position without a long "float."

5. When working each color change, look ahead to see where the corresponding change occurs on the next row. If it will occur before the current change, you can twist the colors every one or two stitches up to that position on the current row, then leave the old color where it will be required on the next row.
6. If you forget tips 4 and 5 and find you have left some long floats, you can probably catch them in when you run in the ends!

FINISHING TOUCHES

Details of knitted motifs may be enhanced with embroidery, or small motifs added entirely in this way. Simple embroidery stitches, such as chain stitch, may be worked in wool or another compatible yarn but are often susceptible to damage when worn—swiss darning as described below is much more robust. Pompoms and other decorations such as simple braids may be made from wool, or braids and cords purchased ready-made. Beads may be sewn onto a finished garment, although knitting them in as the work proceeds, as below, is much more secure.

SWISS DARNING

The technique of swiss darning (duplicate stitch) matches the appearance of stockinette stitch. Choose a yarn of the same thickness as that used for the knitting, or even a little heavier, to cover the knitted stitches completely. Use a blunt-tipped needle, or tapestry needle, of a suitable size and take care not to split the knitted stitches with the needle point but pass the needle between the knitted strands.

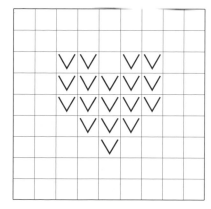

MOTIF FOR SWISS DARNING

Each small square represents one knitted stitch.

 = a knitted stitch, swiss-darned with a contrast color.

STEP 1
Leave a 6 in. (15 cm) tail at the back of the the work when starting the first stitch. (This will be run in later.) Bring the needle up at the base of the stitch to be covered and pass it from right to left under the two threads forming the stitch above. Pull the yarn through.

STEP 2
Re-insert the needle at the base of the stitch, where it first emerged, and pull the excess yarn through to the back, so covering one knitted stitch. Do not work too tightly or the knitting will be distorted.

STEP 3
When working several rows of swiss darning, begin at the base of the motif, work one row from right to left and the next from left to right, ending at the top of the motif. When the embroidery is complete, run in the yarn ends on the wrong side of the work.

Making a pompom

Use a pair of compasses to draw two circles of the size required for the pompom onto cardboard, with a small circle at the center of each. Cut out the circles, cut a small wedge out of each circle, and cut out the central holes. The two pieces should be the same.

STEP 1 Place the two pieces together. Beginning at the outer edge, wind the yarn around the circles until they are completely covered and the central hole is almost full, ending at the outer edge. Cut the yarn. The more yarn you wind, the fatter the finished pompom will be.

STEP 2 Slip the point of your scissors between the two layers of cardboard and cut through the yarn all around.

STEP 3

Take a 12 in. (30 cm) length of yarn and tie it tightly round the center between the two layers of cardboard. Remove the cardboard circles—if you are careful, you can use them again. Trim off any ragged ends and use the tying thread to attach the pompom.

TIP

Make multi-colored pompoms by winding two or three different yarns together.

KNITTING WITH BEADS

It is most important to choose beads that will fit easily onto the knitting yarn.

STEP 1

Before beginning to knit, thread all the beads required onto the ball of yarn, using a needle that fits comfortably through the beads. If the yarn runs out before the bead knitting is complete, simply thread the remaining beads onto a new ball in the same way.

If the needle threaded with the yarn is too big for the beads, use a knotted length of finer thread to lead the yarn through.

STEP 2 Each

bead is normally placed in front of a slip stitch on a right-side row: at the position required, bring the yarn to the front of the work, passing it between the needles, and slip the next stitch knitwise onto the right needle.

TIPS

1. On the row following a row with beads, make sure each bead is at the front of the work before working into the slip stitch that holds it in place.
2. When working with small beads, the slip stitches may be worked purlwise to avoid a twisted stitch that will not be hidden by the bead.

STEP 3 Push a

bead up the yarn in front of the slip stitch, close to the right needle. Take the yarn to the back of the work, passing it between the needles, and continue working to the position for the next bead.

Simple beaded pattern requires a multiple of 4 sts, plus 3.

Row 1 (RIGHT-SIDE ROW) K1, *place bead, k3, repeat from * to last 2 sts, place bead, k1.
Row 2 P.
Row 3 K.
Row 4 P.
Row 5 K3, *place bead, k3, repeat from * to end.
Rows 6 TO 8 Repeat rows 2 to 4
Repeat these 8 rows.

CHILD'S SWEATER

This chunky sweater is styled very simply with drop shoulders and no armhole shaping, so you can concentrate on the intarsia rabbit motif. The eyes, nose, and whiskers are embroidered after knitting is complete, and a pompon tail added to complete the picture.

SIZES

to fit chest	20	22	24	26	in.
	51	56	61	66	cm
actual measurement	23	25	27½	29½	in.
	58.5	63.5	70	75	cm
length to shoulder	12½	13¾	16	18	in.
	31	35	40.5	45.5	cm
sleeve seam	8	9¾	11½	13	in.
	20	25	29	33	cm

MATERIALS

SIRDAR SNUGGLY CHUNKY (APPROX. 80 YDS/73 M PER 50 G BALL)

COLOR A bluebell (shade 354) 4[5 6 7] 50-g balls

COLOR B white (shade 251) 1[1 1 1]

COLOR C small amount of dark gray yarn for embroidery

NEEDLES sizes 10½ (6½ mm) and 9 (5½ mm)

set of 4 double-pointed needles, or short circular needles, sizes 9 (5½ mm) and 10½ (6½ mm)

2 stitch holders

GAUGE

Required gauge over stockinette is 14 sts and 19 rows to 4 in. (10 cm). Using size 10½ (6½ mm) needles, cast on 20 sts and work 24 rows stockinette. Measure gauge (pages 50–51). If your gauge is tight, with more sts or rows to 4 in. (10 cm), try another test-piece with larger needles. If your gauge is loose, with fewer sts or rows to 4 in. (10 cm), try again with smaller needles.

ABBREVIATIONS

k—knit; **p**—purl; **rep**—repeat; **st(s)**—stitch(es); **inc**—increase; **m1 tbl**—make 1 through back loop; **k2tog**—knit two together; **SKP**—slip one, knit one pass slip stitch over; **p2tog**—purl two together; **p2tog tbl**—purl 2 together through back loops; **col.**—color; **in.**—inches; **cm**—centimeters.

TIP

Choose a finer yarn for the embroidery, such as DK or worsted weight. Use it double for the swiss darning, to cover the stitches well, and use it singly for the whiskers so they are not too clumsy.

NOTES

1. Instructions in brackets [ ] refer to the 3 larger sizes. Where only one set of figures is given this refers to all sizes.
2. Sweater in photograph is 2nd size.

BACK

Using size 9 (5½ mm) needles and col.A cast on 42[46, 50, 54] sts.

Row 1 *K1, p1, rep from * to end.

Rep this row 3[5, 5, 5] more times. 4[6, 6, 6] rib rows in all.

Change to size 10½ (6½ mm) needles. *

Row 1 K to end.

Row 2 K1, p to last st, k1. Work all wrong side rows of stockinette in this way, with 1 selvage st at each edge.

Rep these 2 rows, 13[16, 20, 24] more times. 28[34, 42, 50] rows of stockinette in all, ending with a p row.

Place a marker at each end of last row. These mark the beginning of the armhole.

Rep rows 1 and 2, 13[13, 14, 15] more times. 26[26, 28, 30] rows in all from markers, ending with a p row. 54[60, 70, 80] stockinette rows in all.

Shape Shoulders

Bind off 6[6, 7, 7] sts at beginning next 2 rows, knitwise on k row, purlwise on p row.

Bind off 6[7, 7, 8] sts at beginning following 2 rows. 18[20, 22, 24] sts remain.

Slip these sts onto a stitch holder and cut yarn leaving a 6 in. (15 cm) tail.

FRONT

Work as given for Back to **.

Work in stockinette as given for Back for 0[6, 10, 14] rows, thus ending with a wrong-side row. (NOTE: for 1st size only, motif begins immediately after rib rows.)

Rabbit Motif

For full instructions on intarsia knitting, see pages 114–116.

From a new ball of col.A, wind off about 4 yds (3.5 m) into a small ball. From the ball of col.B, wind off about 5 yds (4.5 m) into a small ball. These balls will be used later when working the two ears.

Read right-side (k) rows (odd numbers) from right to left, and wrong-side (p) rows from left to right:

Chart row 1 With ball of col.A already in use, k 10[12, 14, 16] sts, using large ball of col.B, k 18 sts, using new ball of col.A, k 14[16, 18, 20] sts

to end.

Chart row 2 Using col.A, k1, p 13[15, 17, 19], change to col.B, p 19 sts, change to col.A, p 8[10, 12, 14], k1.

Continue in this way, reading from successive chart rows, keeping motif correct.

On chart row 15, under rabbit's front leg, carry col.A across back of 7 sts, twisting yarns twice (page 109) to prevent a long "float."

When chart row 28[28, 32, 36] is complete, place a marker at each end of last row.

On chart row 33, use ball of col.B already in work for sts of first ear, join in small ball of col.A for sts between ears and join in small ball of col.B for sts of second ear.

Continue until chart row 45 is complete.

Change to col.A and stockinette, beginning with a p row work 1[1, 5, 11] rows. 46[52, 60, 70] rows in all from last rib row.

Shape Front Neck: First Side

1st neck row K 17[18, 20, 21] sts, turn. Work on these sts only:

2nd neck row P2tog, p to last st, k1.

3rd neck row K to last 2 sts, k2tog.

Rep 2nd and 3rd neck rows 1[1, 2, 2] more times.

1st and 2nd Sizes Only

Work 2nd neck row once again.

All Sizes

12[13, 14, 15] sts remain. Work 2[2, 3, 3] more rows, ending p row. 54[60, 70, 80] rows in all from last rib row, matching Back at beginning of shoulder shaping.

Shape Shoulder

Next row Bind off 6[6, 7, 7] sts knitwise, k to end.

Following row P to end.

Bind off remaining 6[7, 7, 8] sts knitwise. Cut yarn leaving a 12 in. (30 cm) tail.

Shape Front Neck: Second Side

With right side of Front facing, slip 8[10, 10, 12] sts at center onto a stitch holder and rejoin col.A at right of remaining 17[18, 20, 21] sts.

1st neck row K to end.

2nd neck row P to last 2 sts, p2tog tbl.

3rd neck row SKP, k to end.

Rep 2nd and 3rd neck rows, 1[1, 2, 2] more times.

1st and 2nd Sizes Only

Work 2nd neck row once again.

All Sizes

12[13, 14, 15] sts remain. Work 3[3, 4, 4] more
rows, ending k row.

Shape Shoulder

Next row Bind off 6[6, 7, 7] sts purlwise, p to
end.

Following row K to end.

Bind off remaining 6[7, 7, 8] sts purlwise. Cut yarn
leaving a 12 in. (30 cm) tail.

SLEEVE MAKE 2

Using size 9 (5½ mm) needles and col.A cast on
26[26, 28, 28] sts.

Row 1 *K1, p1, rep from * to end.

Rep this row 5 more times. 6 rib rows in all.

Change to size 10½ (6½ mm) needles.

Shape Sleeve

Inc row 1 K1, m1 tbl, k to last st, m1 tbl, k1.
28[28, 30, 30] sts.

Work 5 rows stockinette, beginning and ending p
row with selvage sts, as for Back.

Rep these 6 rows, 3[5, 5, 6] more times. 34[38, 40,
42] sts. 24[36, 36, 42] rows of stockinette in all
from last rib row.

Work inc row 1 again. 36[40, 42, 44] sts.

Continue in stockinette beginning p row until
Sleeve measures 8[9¾, 11½, 13] in./20[25, 29,
33] cm in all from cast-on edge, or length
required, ending with a p row.

Bind off loosely.

ASSEMBLY

Run in all yarn ends from motif (page 116). Block
pieces using water-spray method (page 41).

Work embroidery on motif as shown on chart. See
pages 117–118 for swiss darning. Join shoulder
seams with backstitch (pages 44–45) using ends
left for this purpose. Fold one Sleeve in half
lengthwise to find center of top edge. Match
this point to shoulder seam. Match top corners
of Sleeve to markers on side edges of Back and
Front. Join armhole seam (page 44). Join top
edge of other Sleeve to armhole in same way.
Join side and sleeve seams using mattress stitch
(pages 42–43), taking selvage sts into seams.

CREW NECK

With right side of work facing, using set of 4

double-pointed needles or circular needle size 9 (5½ mm) needles and col.A, begin at right shoulder seam: k across 18[20, 22, 24] sts from holder at back neck; pick up and k 10[10, 11, 11] sts from first side of front neck shaping; k across 8[10, 10, 12] sts from holder at center front and pick up and k 10[10, 11, 11] sts from second side of front neck shaping. 46[50, 54, 58] sts. (See pages 74–76 for working in the round and pages 46–47 for picking up sts).

Round 1 *K1, p1, rep from * to end.
Rep this round 3 more times.
Change to a size 10½ (6½ mm) needle and bind off in k and p as established.
Using col.B make a pompom (pages 119–120) about 2 in. (5 cm) across. Sew in place for rabbit's tail.
Run in any remaining yarn ends along seams.

CHART FOR FRONT

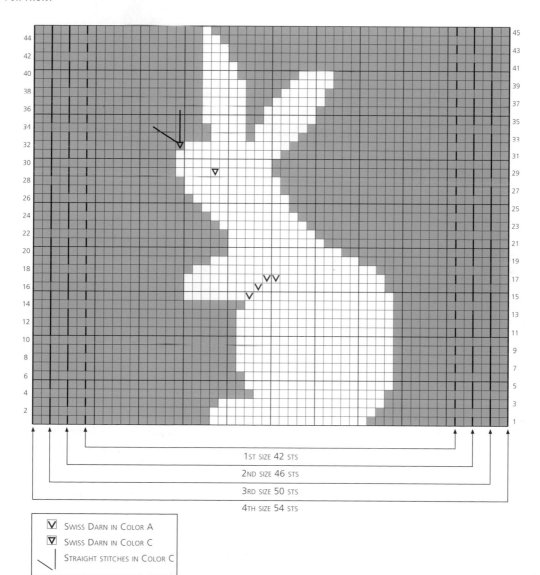

1ST SIZE 42 STS
2ND SIZE 46 STS
3RD SIZE 50 STS
4TH SIZE 54 STS

☑ SWISS DARN IN COLOR A
▽ SWISS DARN IN COLOR C
╲ STRAIGHT STITCHES IN COLOR C

GLOSSARY

2-ply, 3-ply, 4-ply Knitting with two colors in the same row.

Backstitch A firm sewing stitch.

Binding off Fastening off stitches so they do not unravel.

Block, blocking Treating a piece of knitting to set its shape.

Bouclé yarn A fancy yarn with a knobbly effect.

Button band or button border A piece, knitted sideways or lengthwise, to which buttons are sewn.

Buttonhole band or buttonhole border A piece, knitted sideways or lengthwise, with buttonholes worked as knitting proceeds.

Cable needle A short, double-pointed knitting needle for working cables.

Cable A group of stitches crossed over another group of stitches.

Casting on Making new stitches on a needle.

Chunky A heavy-weight yarn.

Circular needle A long, double-pointed knitting needle with a flexible center section, used for working in the round, or working large numbers of stitches.

Cuff The lower border of a sleeve.

Decreasing Working stitches together to reduce their number.

Double-pointed needle A knitting needle with a point at each end.

Duplicate stitch Another name for swiss darning.

Dye lot number Indicates the exact dye bath used to dye the yarn in question, not just the shade.

Ease The difference between the body measurement and the measurement of a garment.

Eyelet A small hole for a buttonhole or as part of a lace stitch pattern.

Fair Isle Knitting with two colors in the same row.

Fingering A fine-weight yarn (similar to 2-ply and 3-ply).

Float The strand of yarn left at the wrong side of the work when stranding.

Fully-fashioned shaping Shaping emphasized by working decreases (or increases) two or more stitches in from the edge of the work.

Garter stitch Formed by working all stitches as knit on every row, or all stitches as purl on every row.

Gauge The number of stitches and rows to a given measurement.

Hank A coil of yarn.

Increasing Making extra stitches.

Intarsia The technique of "picture" knitting.

Knitwise As when knitting a stitch.

Long stitch A stitch made by wrapping the yarn twice around the needle.

Mattress stitch The stitch used for the invisible seam.

Multiple The number of stitches required for one pattern repeat.

Needle gauge A small metal or plastic sheet with holes of different sizes, labeled with needle sizes, for checking the size of knitting needles.

Pattern repeat The stitches and rows which must be repeated to form a stitch pattern.

Pattern A stitch pattern or a set of instructions for making a garment.

Point protector A plastic device to protect the point of a knitting needle.

Purlwise As when purling a stitch.

Raglan A sleeve and armhole shaping that slopes from the armhole to the neck edge.

Reverse stockinette stitch Stockinette stitch worked with the purl side as the right side.

Rib stitches or ribbing Various combinations of knit and purl stitches, arranged to form vertical lines.

Right and left (when describing parts of a garment) The terms that describe where the garment part will be when worn, e.g. the right sleeve is the sleeve worn on the right arm, not the sleeve on the right when the garment is viewed from the front.

Right side The side of the work that will be outside the garment when worn.

Ring marker A small split ring of metal or plastic, slipped onto a stitch or onto a needle to mark a particular position in the work.

Seam The join made when two pieces of knitting are sewn together.

Seed stitch A stitch pattern with a "dotted" appearance.

Selvage stitch The first or last stitch of a row worked in a different way to the rest of the row, to make a decorative edge, or a firm, neat edge for seaming.

Set-in sleeve A sleeve and armhole shaping where the armhole is curved to take a curved sleeve head.

Shaping Increasing or decreasing the number of stitches to form the shape required.

Slip stitch A stitch slipped from one needle to the other without working into it, or a simple sewing stitch taking one strand from one edge and one strand from the other.

Stitch holder A device used for holding stitches temporarily.

Stockinette stitch Formed by working one row of knit stitches, one row of purl stitches, and repeating these two rows.

Stranding Carrying a color to a new position across the wrong side of the work.

Swiss darning Embroidering over individual knitted stitches with another color.

Tapestry needle A sewing needle with a blunt tip and a large eye.

Twist A single stitch crossed over another stitch.

Twisting Carrying a color across the wrong side of several stitches in another color, twisting the two colors at intervals.

Worsted A medium-weight yarn (similar to double knitting).

Wrong side The side of the work that will be inside the garment when worn.

ABBREVIATIONS & SYMBOLS

Common Knitting Abbreviations

These are some of the most common knitting abbreviations. Note that different design sources use upper and lower case letters for many of these abbreviations.

alt alternate
beg beginning
C cable or cross
C6L cable to left (page 96)
C6R cable to right (page 97)
CC contrast color
col color
cm(s) centimeter (s)
cont continue
dec(s) decrease(s), decreasing
DK double knitting
dpn double pointed needle(s)
foll following
g, gr or gm gram
g st garter stitch (page 25)
in(s) inch(es)
inc(s) increase(s), increasing
incl include, including
k knit (page 24)
kbf knit into back and front of same stitch
kfb knit into front and back of same stitch (page 62)
k2tog knit 2 together (page 67)
kwtw knit winding yarn twice (page 101)
LH left hand
LT left twist (page 98)

MB make bobble (page 103)
MC main color
m1 make one ("lift and knit" as page 91)
m1 tbl or m1b make one ("lift and knit through back loop" as page 63)
oz ounce
p purl (page 26)
pat or patt pattern
pbf purl into back and front of same stitch
pfb purl into front and back of same stitch
psso pass slip stitch over
p2tog purl 2 together (page 68)
pwtw purl winding yarn twice (page 103)
rem remaining
rep repeat
rev st st reverse stockinette stitch (page 28)
RH right hand
rib ribbing
rd(s) or rnd(s) round(s)
rs right side (of work)
RT right twist (page 99)
sk skip
SK2togpsso slip 1, knit 2 together, use left needle to lift slipped stitch over new stitch and off right needle, leaving one stitch on right needle (two stitches decreased)

SKP (or sl 1, k1, psso) slip 1, knit 1, pass slip stitch over (page 65)
sl slip
sl st slip stitch
sp(s) space(s)
SSK slip 2 stitches knitwise, one at a time to right needle. Wrap yarn round right needle and use left needle to lift both slipped stitches over yarn and off right needle, leaving one stitch on right needle
st(s) stitch(es)
st st stockinette stitch (page 28)
tbl through back loop(s)
tog together
ws wrong side (of work)
wyib with yarn in back, as if to knit (page 102)
wyif with yarn in front, as if to purl (page 102)
yb or ybk yarn to the back between needles
yd yard
yf or yfwd yarn to the front between needles
yo or yon yarn over needle to make extra stitch (page 89)

Common Symbols

Sometimes stitch patterns are shown in chart form instead of as written instructions. A chart represents the appearance of the right side of the work and is normally accompanied by its own key. The use of charts to present stitch patterns is an international system that bypasses any language problems. Each square on the chart represents one stitch, and each line of squares represents one row. Rows are numbered from the bottom of the chart to the top, in the order in which they should be worked. Odd-numbered rows are usually right-side rows, numbered to the right of the chart. Even-numbered rows are usually wrong-side rows, numbered to the left. Here is a key to the most common chart symbols used.

 selvage stitch

 stockinette stitch, k on rs row, p on ws row

 reverse stockinette stitch

 yarn over (yo)

 slip stitch knitwise (wyib on rs rows, wyif on ws rows)

 make one through back loop (m1 tbl)

 make one (m1)

 K2tog on rs row, p2tog on ws row

 SKP on rs row, p2tog tbl on ws row

 P2tog on rs row, k2tog on ws row

 P2tog tbl on rs row, k2tog tbl on ws row

 make bobble (MB)

 right twist (RT)

 left twist (LT)

 cable 4 stitches to right (C4R)

 cable 4 sts to left (C4L)

(Other cables are represented in a similar way)

INDEX

A
abbreviations 34, 54,127
accessories 15

B
Baby Afghan 48–49
backstitch seam 44–45
beads, knitting with 120
binding off 29–30
block pattern 71
blocking 40–41, 79
    board 40
bobbins 15, 114
bobble dots 104
buttonholes 82–83
buttons 82

C
cable 96–97, 106
casting on 20–23
charts: for Fair Isle 112
    for intarsia 115, 125
    symbols 127
checkers 48
chevrons 93
Child's Sweater 122–125
crochet hook method 57–58

D
decreasing 65–70
double cable panel 100

E
ease 53

F
Fair Isle 107–109
Fair Isle Sweater 110–113
Family Sweater 72–73
fully-fashioned shaping 71

G
garter stitch 24–25, 34, 38–39
    random rows 34
    stripes 48
gauge 50–52

H
honeycomb 100

I
in-the-round knitting 74–76, 80
increasing 62–65
intarsia 114–116, 122–125

J
joining in 31

K
knit stitch 24–25
    see also garter stitch
knotted lines 93

L
lace patterns 89–93
Lady's Lacy Vest 94–95
lifted eyelet 91, 92–93
little posts 48
little squares 37
little tails 104
little towers 93
long stitch waves 103

M
mattress stitch seam 42–43, 59
measurements 52–53
measuring work 55
mistakes, correcting 57–58

N
neckbands 46, 81
needles 14
    cable 15, 96
    changing 55, 62
    choosing 16
    circular 14, 74–75, 81
    double-pointed 14, 74, 76, 81
    holding 19
    protecting 14, 15, 70
    sizes 14, 16, 50

O
order of knitting 55

P
paired decreases 67
pattern, keeping correct 71
pattern repeats 35, 107
patterns: abbreviations 34, 54, 127
    instructions 54
    using 52–55
pocket 84, 87
pompom 119–120
pouch see pocket
purl stitch 26–27
    binding off 30

R
raindrops 100
rib stitches 35–37
    binding off 30
    broken 36, 72–73
ridge stitch 34
ring marker 15, 76
row count 15, 55, 106

S
scarf 38–39
seams 41–45
selvages 42, 59, 108, 113
sizing a garment 52–53
slip knot 17–18
slip stitch bricks 103
stitch holders 15, 56, 84
stitch multiples 35

stitch and row seam 44
stitches: caterpillar 37
    garter 24–25, 34, 38–39
    holding 56
    knit 24–25
    long 101
    moss 37
    picking up 46–47
    purl 26–27
    reverse stockinette 28, 34
    reversed 37
    rib 35–37, 72–73
    ridge 34
    seed 37
    slip 102
    stockinette 28, 34, 37
    textured 101–103
    trinity 104
    twist 98–99, 100
    uneven 25
stockinette stitch 28, 34, 37
    reverse 28, 34
storing: work 70
    yarn 12
stranding 107–108
Striped Garter Scarf 38–39
stripes 38–39, 78–79
swiss darning 117–118

T
tails, running in 42, 45, 116
Tank Top 60–61
Toddler Top 86
twisting 109, 116
twists 98–99, 100

U
uneven rows 28
uneven stitches 25
unraveling method 58

Y
yarn: choosing 16
    ends see tails
    holding 19
    joining in 31
    needles 15, 41, 45, 116, 117
    position 35
    for seams 42
    space-dyed 95
    storing 12
    substituting 51
    types 10–11, 50
    weights 11, 12
    winding 11–12
yarn over 62, 82, 89–90, 92